VOICES
OF THE ELDERS

Huu-ay-aht Histories and Legends

KATHRYN BRIDGE
and
KEVIN NEARY

VICTORIA · VANCOUVER · CALGARY

Heritage House Publishing Company Ltd.
heritagehouse.ca

Library and Archives Canada Cataloguing in Publication
Bridge, Kathryn Anne, 1955–
  Voices of the elders: Huu-ay-aht histories and legends / Kathryn Bridge and Kevin Neary.

(Amazing stories)
Previously published in 2004 under the title: Extraordinary accounts of Native life on the West Coast.
Includes some text in Huu-ay-aht.
Includes bibliographical references and index.
Issued also in electronic formats.
ISBN 978-1-927051-94-8

1. Nootka Indians—Folklore. 2. Nootka mythology. I. Neary, Kevin II. Bridge, Kathryn Anne, 1955–. Extraordinary accounts of Native life on the West Coast. III. Title. IV. Series: Amazing stories (Victoria, B.C.)

E99.N85B75 2013   398.2'08997955   C2013-900038-0

Series editor: Lesley Reynolds
Proofreader: Liesbeth Leatherbarrow

Cover photo: A carved Huu-ay-aht ancestor housepost on the banks of the Pachena River at Anacla. Courtesy of www.ourbc.com

MIX
Paper from
responsible sources
FSC
www.fsc.org   FSC® C016245

The interior of this book was produced on 30% post-consumer recycled paper, processed chlorine free and printed with vegetable-based inks.

Heritage House acknowledges the financial support for its publishing program from the Government of Canada through the Canada Book Fund (CBF), Canada Council for the Arts and the province of British Columbia through the British Columbia Arts Council and the Book Publishing Tax Credit.

 Canadian Patrimoine
Heritage canadien

 Canada Council   Conseil des Arts
for the Arts   du Canada

BRITISH COLUMBIA
ARTS COUNCIL

17 16 15 14 13 1 2 3 4 5
Printed in Canada

The authors dedicate this book to Huu-ay-aht colleagues, elders and friends of the past and present.

Contents

Map Key

- - - - Traditional Huu-ay-aht territory

■ The 13 Indian Reserves assigned to the Huu-ay-aht by the government

■ Territory regained in 2011 through the Maa-nulth Treaty

Alberni Inlet

○ Yashitk'o'a
Coleman Creek

BARKLEY SOUND

Numukamis

○ Wihata
Sarita Lake

○ Keekee'hinkook

Sarita River

N'aqowis

Cha'pis   Ots'o'a

Nanaskivis   Bamfield
Kee'hin

Cape Beale   Ch'ima'tokoso'a
Clutus   Anacla

○ Malsit

Pachena
Point

VANCOUVER
ISLAND

MAP AREA

Luh'taa ○
Tsusiat

PACIFIC OCEAN

N
W   E
S

0   5   10   KILOMETRES

Prologue

THE EARTH SHOOK AND THE sky darkened as clouds obscured the full moon. Trees swayed, their branches brushing against one another. From below was heard a sound that seemed almost primal, a deep, penetrating moan. And then came the silence. An eerie aloneness, a moment that stretched into two, and then three—an emptiness when the comforting sounds of the world ceased and an expectation grew. Where was the breeze? Where was the lapping of the waves on the beach? Where were the geese and the owls in the forest?

And then it began. Beneath it all was movement, a sliding, an inertia and a melting. In a flash the subtleties became reality, the sliding intensified and the sand melted beneath the houses. The clouds parted and the moonlight revealed a *glistening world. Liquid poured from the beach, from the forest floor and the meadow. It mixed with the earth, which was suddenly porous. Everything slid within; the houses sank into the soup without a whimper. Not a voice was heard.*

Silence again and an overwhelming expectation. Twinkling in the moonlight far from the shore was a wall, 20 metres high and moving steadily toward the land. Behind it was a void, and before it was absence. Within it was a force unimaginable. When it hit the beach, the wave did not stop; it climbed over the rocks and the bushes, over the hemlock and fir and cedar trees, snapping them instantly. When the wave drew back, it pulled with it all the broken world, stripping the land of everything. The people of Luh'taa were no more.

Introduction

THERE IS A SPECIAL PLACE on the west coast of Vancouver Island. It is a combination of rocky cliffs fronting onto the wild Pacific Ocean, of sheltered beaches, bays and estuaries, lakes, mountains and forests. Geographically, this area is located on the southeastern shores of Barkley Sound, stretching east to Coleman Creek and then southward along the Pacific coastline towards Clo-oose. Inland, the area encompasses the length of the Sarita and Pachena Rivers and their lakes. The landscape is plentiful and supports a wide variety of plants and animals. The ocean abounds with all manner of plant life, crustaceans, fishes and sea mammals. Over the millennia, the rivers and streams have supported plentiful runs of salmon. This place is the ancestral home of the people of the Huu-ay-aht First Nation, who have lived there since the beginning of time. This book is their story, written from their perspective, about the creation of their world and the events that have occurred since the beginning, as well as those that took place after the first "outsiders" came to their shores.

The Huu-ay-aht are part of the larger culture of Nuu-chah-nulth–speaking peoples of western Vancouver Island. Their world includes relationships with neighbouring First Nations, sharing the abundance of foods found in their territories. Over the centuries they have changed and adapted as natural events and those caused by man have presented challenges. For thousands of years, the Huu-ay-aht lived on the land and sea according to age-old traditions and practices. The ocean supplied fish, whales, seals, otters and shellfish. The forests of tall, strong trees provided wood for houses, for carving canoes and for weaving baskets and rope. The deer and elk, the berries, fruits and edible plants provided nourishment. What the Huu-ay-aht could not harvest in their own territory, they purchased, traded or bartered with other First Nations along the coast and inland.

The arrival of the outsiders, beginning with explorers such as Captain James Cook in 1778, initiated a period that forever changed the world of coastal First Nations. The Nuu-chah-nulth word for these outsiders is mamatni, meaning "those whose houses float about on the water"—an appropriate description for a people who were initially encountered lost in the fog and unaware of where they were.

Today, the Huu-ay-aht remain a strong people, assured of their heritage, protective of their territories and traditions. They live in modern times, yet remain grounded in the knowledge of their own ways. Their history has, until recently, been mostly an oral tradition, passed down through the generations. They did not create books for others to read, but kept their knowledge among their own. Times have changed. In the last few decades, the Huu-ay-aht and neighbouring Nuu-cha-nulth First Nations have worked hard to move their people forward and enable change from within. In 2000 the Huu-ay-aht built and celebrated the opening of the House of Huu-ay-aht at Anacla. This community facility is evocative of their "big houses" of the past.

In 2009 the Huu-ay-aht successfully concluded an agreement under the British Columbia Treaty Commission process, and two years later they enacted their own legislative authority via a modern treaty. The Huu-ay-aht now legally govern themselves and have jurisdiction over lands much larger than the 19th-century reserves previously allotted to them, and which they did not legally own. Their own vision statement summarizes their future path: "We, the Huu-ay-aht people, envision a proud, self-governing sovereign Nation. 'Isaak' [Respect] will guide us as we work together to establish a healthy, prosperous, self-sustaining community where our culture, language, spirituality and economy flourish for the benefit of all Huu-ay-aht." It is well past the time when we outsiders should learn more about this First Nation whose citizenship and rights are now enshrined in their own legislation and whose people move proudly forward, once again in control of their own destiny.

The information in this book comes directly from Huu-ay-aht sources. In most cases, Huu-ay-aht place names and personal names are used, but in some cases, in the interest of clarity for a general audience, the anglicized versions also appear. A glossary of Huu-ay-aht place names is included at the end of the book. We have adapted Huu-ay-aht accounts—about the old times, about their ways of doing things and about events in the past—from a variety of sources, principally from translations of interviews given by elders to anthropologists and others who sought them out. In some cases, we have woven together the threads from different versions of stories and from different speakers for a better narrative result.

The foremost source was a chief named Louie Nookmiis (1881–1964). Chief Louie was hereditary chief of the Huu-ay-aht, and his lineage is documented back through the famous Chief Tliishin from Kee'hin. He provided information about Huu-ay-aht culture and history to government officials and others in the early 20th century, then later to linguists, anthropologists and people interested in and respectful of Huu-ay-aht history. The tape-recorded stories he told to Eugene Arima in 1964, just a few months before his death, provide the basis for many of the chapters presented here. Chief Louie played a significant role in documenting the culture and traditions of his people. He recounted Huu-ay-aht history as he had learned it from his father and his father's father. His oral accounts of history include not only events of the last 200 years or so, but encompass truths about ancestors and the Huu-ay-aht world view.

Other elders shared Huu-ay-aht history with interested outsiders as well. Among them were Klamahouse, born in 1826 and an elder when Chief Louie was a young boy; Hyna'um (also known as Mr. Bengi), who in 1922 told Alfred Carmichael stories about his youth in the village of Kee'hin; Sa'sawatin and his wife, Yima'uk, who collaborated with Hyan'um to provide accounts of the great flood; and William, a Tseshaht man of Huu-ay-aht ancestry who was born in either 1869 or 1870. William's understanding of the history of the Barkley Sound tribes is apparent in the variety of accounts he related to anthropologist Edward Sapir in 1913 and 1914. More recently, other Huu-ay-aht elders have added to these important narratives.

The Huu-ay-aht Chiefs and Council approved the writing of the first edition of this book and also this new edition, recognizing that it is intended for a general audience, not for the specialist, and that it is to serve as an introduction to the complex and rich history of their people.

1

Chief Louie and
the Four Great Spirits

CHIEF LOUIE NOOKMIIS LOOKED OUT on the Land, across the sturdy golden grasses that crept out at the edge of the salal and fir forest, to the cobble beach and the waves that rolled gently against the sloping pebbles. His gaze swept out across the ocean, where deep beneath its surface lay hidden the wealth of plants and creatures that provided food for his people. The sun's fading light cast the waters in a rosy iridescence, while far offshore a whale breached, spouting spray from its blowhole. The unique expiration of water and air could be heard clearly as the sound travelled in the afternoon peacefulness.

"Hishuk Taswak," Chief Louie murmured in response. "All is one, all is one." And he turned back to his chair, which stood on the lawn in front of Aguilar House near Bamfield Inlet. He sat for a while, silent and thoughtful, turning inwards in preparation. Much depended upon his accuracy, his recall and his thoroughness. To him was given the responsibility of knowing the ways of his people and teaching those ways to others. The younger generation listened to him as he spoke, but they did not all hear, hear in that special way so necessary for the history to remain whole, to be transferred from father to son, and to his son and his son's son.

"We must use what we have," he reminded himself once more and turned to the anthropologist beside him. "All right, I'm ready. Start the recorder." And Chief Louie Nookmiis, hereditary chief of the Huu-ay-aht people, began to speak.

"Four Great Spirits keep our world," he said, pausing briefly to select his words. "They give shape to all we see and all we are. They are the beginning and the always. They define what we see and together they create the Huu-ay-aht World. These Great Spirits are Land, Above, Horizon and Undersea.

"The Great Spirit of the Land rules over all the oceans and rivers and mountains, lakes, forests and beaches. The tiniest drops of clear dew on the grasses, the new soft green needles on the fir trees, the rounded pebbles on the beach, are all small parts of this Great Spirit.

"The stars in the night sky, the moon, the sun and the

warm light in the summer all come from the Great Spirit Above. As does the wind and the rain, soft in summer but cold and lashing in winter. Rain that fills up the Land makes our rivers strong and the oceans plentiful. Above controls clouds and storms and the healing sunshine.

"Horizon is the doorway for travellers, ever-changing as we move on the Land. Horizon tells us about what is coming. Look out upon the ocean and see where the world ends. Horizon is the Great Spirit who controls the boundaries. When we look out over the ocean—as far as is possible—we see the beginning of Horizon; when the mountains touch the Sky and where the Land meets the Sky, when the eye can see no farther, this is Horizon.

"The Great Spirit Undersea directs the oceans and the tides, and its waters provide food for all the creatures of the Land and the Sky. Undersea is powerful—as powerful as the waves that dash the shores and smooth each pebble and rock on the beach. Undersea is mysterious, for it houses life that can only survive in water and in darkness, deep below.

"In the beginning our world was the home for supernatural creatures. The Thunderbird, the Giant Shark, Ya'i (the spirits of the mountains) and the Pok mis (the wild people of the woods) are just some of these. There were no people the way we are today. The animals also lived in this world, but they were different, they had two selves. The coverings of the animals—their fur, their scales and their feathers—were like clothing. Whenever the animals took their clothing off they became Kuu-us, that is, they became like people. The animals roamed all around the land and had homes right in their territories. Bears, the elk and the deer, raccoons, minks, beaver—all had homes and houses. The birds in the sky all had homes on the land. Whenever they entered their homes, they took their clothing off and suddenly transformed into a Kuu-us, such as us, the way we are now.

"Eventually, some of the animals decided they liked to stay as Kuu-us, and these ones became our first ancestors. This was a long time ago. My grandfather told me this is how our people were created. The first man was named Nutchkoa and the first woman, Hominiki. Our carvers depicted their forms on the welcome figures on the house at which I was born, at Kee'hin."

The anthropologist turned off the tape recorder, and both men looked at each other as they rose from their chairs.

"Could we have a short break now?" the anthropologist asked.

"Just for a minute," Chief Louie replied. "I've just barely got started, and I have so much more to relate. Now is the time for me to tell you what I know, what my people know, about who we are and how our world is made."

"All right, I'll just have a quick stretch and let's get back to it."

Chief Louie Nookmiis on the porch of his house in Bamfield Inlet in 1963. He is holding some fur-sealing spearheads. HUU-AY-AHT FIRST NATION

After a few more minutes, the two settled back. Family members arrived and they, too, settled themselves down in preparation for a good listen. And then Chief Louie picked up the thread of his story.

"All this creation happened at Useless Inlet. It began there, in the shadow of the Thunderbird Mountain and then gradually spread throughout the land. The birds and deer, bear, mink, elk and other animals who wanted to remain as animals did so. They put their hides back on and returned to the forest. The others took off their hides, never to replace them. They became human and no longer shared lives with the animals. This was the first separation.

"Much had to be learned to be human. We had to learn to hunt these animals in order to feed ourselves. We had to hunt the animals and to kill them and to eat. We had new bodies and learned about the differences between women and men. We had to learn how to produce babies and about the roles of mothers and fathers, and then grandparents, in the upbringing of children. We learned to respect and carefully look after all our resources. We learned to only catch what we needed, to conserve our sea resources and take only the species we needed for food. This was all taught at Useless Inlet and then sent throughout the Land."

Chief Louie then glanced at the faces of those listening. It was to his own family that he now spoke.

"When I was young, I heard about Ko'o'shin. Ko'o'shin is the Raven. This story was told to me by an elder whose name was Klamahouse. This is what he told me. This is from the days when animals and people were not yet separated. The Raven was chief of the village between Bamfield and Sarita on the ocean. When Ko'o'shin was at home he appeared as an ordinary human being. When he travelled, he donned his coat of black feathers. Ko'o'shin had two children, a boy and a girl, but he was widowed and lonely so he resolved to find a new wife. One morning, he put on his coat of black feathers and went outside his house, leaving his children alone. This Raven then flew to many different villages, first to the village of the Ucluelets, then to the village of the Ahousahts, then the Hesquiahts, and then to the Mowachahts, and finally he arrived at a village that lay midway between Nootka and Kyuquot Sounds. He had flown a long distance and was tired. Ko'o'shin lighted on a spruce tree that stood on the bank of a stream near this village. As he rested, a beautiful maiden came out of one of the houses carrying a woven bucket. Behind her raced two young boys who ran down the bank and into the river, where they were instantly transformed into two fish who then leaped and swam about in the water.

"Ko'o'shin called to the maiden, but did not use words. He communicated with the thoughts from his mind. 'Please dip your bucket in the stream under the spruce tree in which I sit, for I am tired and thirsty and would like a drink of cool water.' She understood and dipped her bucket into the stream. As she lifted the bucket up, however, a sudden thirst came upon her and she dipped her hand into the bucket to scoop some water to drink. When she did this, Ko'o'shin shook the branch of the spruce tree and a few needles fell down over the maiden. As she drank, she swallowed one. It was very sharp and it choked her, so she left the bucket and ran back to the house, coughing and sputtering as she went. The girl's father was chief of the tribe, and when his daughter came choking into the house he was in a panic. She began to spit blood and then died. The chief and his wife wailed at the loss. It was a great sorrow.

"After a time, they wrapped her body in a blanket, put the body into a cedar box and tied the box up with a rope of cedar bark. This coffin was then placed in a canoe. The men of the village paddled the canoe across the bay to a point opposite the village. Here they left it. Ko'o'shin watched and flew to the place where the body lay. With his beak he untied the knot on the cedar rope and took the blanket off the face of the dead girl. This Raven had special magic medicine, which he put into her mouth, and the girl began to breathe once more. He spoke to her and said, 'I will marry you and take you to my home.' He then picked her up, for she was very weak, and put her on his back. He cautioned, 'You must keep your eyes closed, for you are not yet strong. We are going home.'

"Ko'o'shin retraced his journey and stopped at each of the villages again, this time to rest. Each time he told the girl to keep her eyes closed. 'If you open your eyes we will fall from the sky. Hold on to me tight, put your arms around my neck and we will fly home.' But really, what Ko'o'shin wanted was that she not know where he was taking her. As they got closer to his village, Ko'o'shin told her a little more about himself, who he was and about his family and village. The last leg of the journey occurred in darkness because the Raven did not want anyone to see that he had a young maiden with him. Finally he reached his house and found the children very hungry, for they'd had no food while he was away. Ko'o'shin made a fire and everyone went to bed.

"The next morning Ko'o'shin flew to a high tree and watched the coming and going in the village. He saw the canoes come in from fishing and watched as the fish were cleaned. When the people left, he flew down and picked up what scraps he could find. That evening he returned home and took off his black coat. He did not bring food for his wife, who was very hungry. 'Why did you not bring food?' she asked, but received no answer. For the Raven did not understand the hunger of one who is not a Transformer.

"One evening he returned home and found his new wife and the children very happy. They all had been eating. Ko'o'shin smelled the odour of fish and sniffed around trying to find it, but he could not. He then left the house. His wife asked the little girl to pass her dish, which she did. It was filled with water, and when the wife put her little finger into this water, a dog salmon came out of her finger. This was a secret. The little girl was instructed not to tell her father that his new wife could make salmon appear from her finger. But later that evening, Ko'o'shin took his daughter with him to the beach to gather wood. He questioned the girl, and she would not tell. Ko'o'shin became very angry and threatened to leave her on a small island that would be submerged at high tide. The child relented and told her father the truth. They returned home and pulled the canoe up on the beach.

"Ko'o'shin then called to his wife. 'Come and swim with me.'

"'Yes,' she replied. 'We will swim tonight. Go to the creek and pile up stones to make a dam so the water will be deeper.'

"Ko'o'shin went out and made four deep pools. That night his wife put her hands in each of the pools, one by one. Each time, dog salmon appeared in the pools. 'Tell all the people to come and take salmon, for there is lots for all.' The people came and took many salmon to smoke for the winter food. Ko'o'shin also took salmon—he took an entire canoe load. He hung them all up to dry and then began to bring in wood for the fire. It took several trips to bring in all the wood. Twice while his arms were filled with wood, his head brushed a salmon, which was hanging up on a drying rack. The second time he became very angry, pulled the salmon off the drying rack and threw it down on the ground. His wife was offended, as she was of the salmon family. All the salmon were insulted and returned to the water again. At the last, his wife, too, turned into a dog salmon and swam away."

By now Chief Louie's listeners had grown in numbers. They sat on the porch, the four stairs leading to the garden and the base of the steps. As he talked, they arrived silently and took their places, all eyes trained on his face. These were stories from long ago, stories that had meaning for each one of them. They waited patiently for the next one to begin.

2

The Great Flood

IMAGINE WHAT WOULD HAPPEN IF the rain would not stop and the seas rose, if water covered the land with no escape from wetness and cold. Imagine the fierce wind ripping through the trees, lashing the rain into stinging pellets of ice while thunder boomed all around. Imagine the panic, the sheer terror of a people whose world suddenly turned against them. Add to this a sudden and continuous darkness. No light and great desperation. This was what happened thousands of years ago. It was a global event of such magnitude that stories recounting this flood are meshed in the fabric of cultures around the world.

Oral traditions, art and written sources worldwide all record a common cataclysmic event: the great flood, when the rains came and did not cease until the known world was covered in water and most living things perished. The Christian biblical account in Genesis features Noah, who built an ark to carry his family and pairs of animals above the flood waters. When the flood waters receded, the ark rested on Mount Ararat. In Mesopotamia, god-king Gilgamesh journeyed to speak with Utnapishtim, the flood survivor whose great boat brought his family and many living things to safety through seven days and nights of rain and darkness. Utnapishtim's boat rested on the top of Mount Nimush and then the flood waters receded. Mayan tradition, as recorded in the Popol Vuh, also tells of the great flood, and Nez Perce history states that the people had to climb Mount Yamustus to survive.

The Great Flood

Chief Louie tells a story of how one group of Huu-ay-aht ancestors survived this flood. The story is set within Barkley Sound at a place called Mugh-yuu.

"Something was wrong at Mugh-yuu because the tide withdrew from the shore. It was not like an ordinary low tide, or the big tides that come in the spring, but a very curious situation. For several days the tide drew out from the beach. In the morning it drew back, and at nighttime it continued to draw back, exposing more and more sand. Everything was drying up because this low tide exposed the sea creatures and sea plants. Blennies flopped in ever-shrinking pools of ocean water trapped in rock crevices. The feather-like plumes of sea anemones, which normally graced the tide pools, were now completely out of the water and shrivelled up. The oyster beds died and the little hermit crabs scuttled about looking for moisture.

"Something was very definitely and terribly wrong. You could see gravel for miles as the tide kept going down. The tide went all the way down to the big halibut banks, which were normally well underwater, some 20 kilometres from shore. Without the water, the reefs looked like mountains and stretched out from a huge gravel creek.

"This was a story passed on to the chiefs. This is something our people witnessed hundreds and hundreds of years ago. These elders of long ago told the people to prepare, 'For the waters will rise again,' they said. They wanted the people to be ready. 'Pull the great canoes down to the beach and tie them together to make them strong, strong enough that we might place all the cedar boards from our houses, and all our belongings into the canoes.'

"Quickly the people gathered all the cedar ropes that they used for whaling and they lashed the canoes tightly together. All at once a cry went out and faces turned towards the dry ocean bed. A small trickle of water now appeared along the exposed sand and gravel. The tide was starting to flow. The elders' prediction was fast becoming reality. Suddenly everyone was gravely serious as the people realized that they were running out of time. Would the waters come slowly and gently refill the bay, or would the tide come back all in one wave? They had no time to lose.

"Nanolinal was the name of the chief who went into the first canoe. Soon all were seated inside the canoes with all the children, animals, food and household supplies around them. By the time the darkness came, the canoes began to drift with the strong surge. Up, up the canoes went on the swell of a gigantic ocean roll. Up, up they went, soon pulled far from their homes. Fierce winds stirred the ocean and threatened to capsize the canoes. Luckily for some, they had tied sealskin floats to the canoes. These are the floats the whalers use to keep a whale's carcass afloat. Those with the floats tied to their canoes survived the storm and ocean turmoil and were saved. But many lives were lost as canoes slipped under the ocean.

"Darkness was all around, and soon in the distance, but seeming ever closer, came great booms which echoed in the night. What terrible being could cause such pounding terror? Finally there came a dawn of sorts, for it was still very black all around. The people who had survived looked out from their canoes to see that they were far off from Sarita and drifting now towards an enormous rock jutting up out of the water. This rock was actually the tip of the great mountain called Kaka'apiya. It was a sacred place. Here lived the Thunderbird, which now flapped its wings, creating a great sound of deafening thunder. The mountain-top was afire. Black ash and rocks spouted in all directions.

The great Sea Serpent was swinging its tail around, hitting the sides of the mountain, causing fire and devastation. No wonder the sky was dark.

"The canoes stayed clear of the Thunderbird and the Sea Serpent. As the fires died down, the Thunderbird ceased its flapping. The people found an outcropping on the rock and tied the canoes to it. Then the water grew still and the wind ceased. Into this silence came a sucking sound, the sound of the tide pulling back. It was so strong that many of the ropes on the canoes snapped like threads. Canoes sank or got caught by the strong current. But a lucky few survived and were able to guide their canoes down with the water. As the water receded, the clouds lifted and the sun appeared. Looking out around them, the people could see extraordinary distances and realized that little had survived this cataclysmic flood.

"A few months later, as they re-established themselves on the land, the people started finding many of the canoes that had sunk, and they travelled great distances looking for survivors. This is how they learned that tribes such as the Nitinat and the Nahmintath had also found refuge, and that when the tide had risen to its fullest, it had reached inland all the way to Sproat Lake, and it was there that canoes from many nations had anchored.

"The land changed greatly from this disaster, and it took time for nature to right itself. Never since has the world experienced such a thing, and hopefully, never again."

The Elderberry Root

In 1922, a Huu-ay-aht elder by the name of Hyna'um (also known as Mr. Bengi), recounted a story of the great flood as it had been told to him by his uncle, Cheepsaw, brother of Tsa'tsa'wist'a. Hyna'um's narration was captured on paper by visitor Alfred Carmichael, who was camping with his family on Brady's Beach, just outside Bamfield. Carmichael heard several of Hyna'um's Huu-ay-aht stories that summer. Theirs was a fortunate collaboration, for some of Hyna'um's accounts proved to be the only surviving versions of important Huu-ay-aht histories. The following version adapts the core of Hyna'um's narrative.

"The flood came at a time when the people stretched all along the coast, and when distinctions between the tribes did not exist. One group of people lived in great numbers at Nitinat. These people were whalers and strong in their canoes. They hunted blue whales and humpback whales. The Nitinat chief, whose name was Cha'ut'sem, lived at the mouth of a creek on the south side of Nitinat Lake, and it is here that the story begins.

"One year, when the winter came, the rains began. It was strong rain, forever rain. The ground could hold no more. The water came into the houses, wetting the living areas and making the food mildew from the damp. The people became very afraid. Cha'ut'sem, too, was afraid, especially when the water came right up to his house. So he told his people: 'We must do this. Strip cedar bark to make ropes.

Make many ropes and make them long and strong. Make more ropes than you have ever done before, because they are needed. Then load all your goods into your canoes and pack them tightly. Leave space for your children and your parents. Then, when all is ready, tie your ropes together to make them very long. Tie one end to an elderberry root. But listen to me, do not tie them to the spruce root, or the hemlock, or the giant cedar, for their roots do not go deep into the earth.'

"When the people heard this they made noise and talked among themselves. The people were very frightened. They did not do as their chief asked. They believed that the mighty trees would be best to hold their canoes, far better than a thin gnarled string of root. So they tied the cedar ropes to the big trees, and the water rose. The rain continued strong, forever rain. Harsh winds blew, and the water beneath their canoes boiled and swirled with its power. The spruce, the cedar and the hemlock roots did not hold to the ground. The trees fell down and broke many of the canoes or else the ropes broke and canoes drifted out to the ocean. Many of the people were killed.

"But Cha'ut'sem, his wife and his four daughters remained safe in their huge canoe, which was six fathoms long. They were spared, for they had tied strong ropes to the elderberry. Although the rain continued and big winds blew, the elderberry did not pull out of the earth. It held the rope fast and provided a safe anchor for the canoe.

After a long while, the water rose very high and covered all the mountains, all except one very high mountain called Kaka'apiya.

"One night, while Cha'ut'sem and his family slept, the canoe floated near to this high mountain and wedged itself into a crook in the rock on the very top of Kaka'apiya. When Cha'ut'sem awoke he saw the Great Spirit sitting in the bow of the canoe. The Great Spirit said to him, 'Do not be afraid. Be of good heart. You and your family will not die. If you sing this song four times, the water will go down.'

"Cha'ut'sem repeated the song four times, and indeed, the water receded, leaving the canoe high and dry on the mountain peak. He waited four days to ensure that the water would not rise again. On the fifth day, Cha'ut'sem and his family returned to their land, but there was no one there. He went to the ocean edge and walked. Some of his people he found at Neah Bay and some at a place between Sooke and Jordan River. These people were few, but they returned to Nitinat with their chief. They built new houses on the oceanfront at Nitinat. But it was many years before the people multiplied and again spread throughout the land."

3

Deep in the Memory:
The Story of Kee'hin

PERPENDICULAR CLIFFS, ERODED, undercut and carved by the waves, rise straight up from the open Pacific Ocean. High above, enormous fir trees grow, bent and resistant to the lashing of the wind and the salt spray of winter storms. On this headland lie the remains of a great fortress. Almost impenetrable salal bushes rise three metres high; their thick and twisted limbs tangle and obscure the landscape. Beneath and intertwined with tree roots lie depressions in the forest floor, confirming the former locations of huge structures. Crumbling earth and stone mounds are the remains of defensive walls. Yes, this was once a great place. But now, steadily and surely, nature reclaims it.

Tucked safely in the lee of this headland is Kee'hin

village. It too lies hidden beneath the ever-growing and encroaching salal, elderberry, ferns and great trees. Kee'hin sits on the southern shore of Barkley Sound, three and a half kilometres southwest of Bamfield, and nine kilometres northeast of Cape Beale, just north of today's popular West Coast Trail and next to Pacific Rim National Park. In 2002 the site of Kee'hin was declared a National Historic Site of Canada.

Kee'hin fortress and village are ancient and have a mighty history. Archaeological evidence confirms that Kee'hin dates back 5,000 years. This was a time when European farmers banded themselves into clans and tribes and built megalithic stone tombs; urban centres developed in the Indus Valley at Mohenjo-Daro and Harappa; Mesopotamian civilization on the Tigris and Euphrates Rivers spawned a priestly society with ziggurats built at Ur; the Yellow River in China held the beginnings of the Hsia Dynasty; and in Egypt, the first of the Great Pyramids at Giza were constructed. Here, at Kee'hin, Huu-ay-aht people also built, but the material they used was wood. In the wet, damp climate of the north Pacific, such material quickly rots. Most of the evidence of the Huu-ay-aht culture—the cedar houses, the carved and ceremonial objects—has not survived through time.

Nevertheless, archaeological research undertaken in recent generations provides hard evidence of human occupation. Barkley Sound has been measured and analyzed to

An artist's rendering of what the central village and fortress of Kee'hin would have looked like circa 1850. ILLUSTRATION BY LORI GRAVES

locate and map land uses and settlements. Within Huu-ay-aht territory alone, over 40 village sites are known, in addition to well over 100 camps used over the centuries for resource harvesting and as lookouts. Six villages had defensive sites like Kee'hin. In the sheltered intertidal areas lie the remains of fish traps made of stone, and there are canoe runs in the beach areas. The forest also preserves telltale signs of its use. Cedar, the tree most utilized for its bark and its wood, was harvested throughout the region. The living trees show signs of bark stripping, and felled trees—chopped and shaped—confirm the widespread use of wood.

Walking through the Kee'hin site today is not easy, for

the forest has taken control, and all is thick with damp and greenery. Even so, the depressions marking large communal houses, which held extended families of 30 or more people, are still visible. Fallen timbers now act as nurse logs for salal and thimbleberry bushes, as well as the fir, hemlock and cedar trees that have encroached on the village site. Behind the village is a hillside lush with gigantic liquorice ferns. At the western edge, scrambling up and over an ancient midden and a tangle of salmonberry bushes, lies the route to the headland and the fortress upon it. It is a forbidding and hidden climb—intentionally so, for village security was crucial.

At its peak, the population of Kee'hin probably reached 500. As the centuries came and went, as war, famine and shifts in the seasonal rounds for resource gathering changed, the population of Kee'hin fluctuated. Depending upon the time of year, the village could be a busy place. Because of its proximity to the open ocean, in the summer Kee'hin absorbed extra people who came to the outer shore of the sound to hunt whales and seals. The great red cedar trees in the forests behind the village were considered some of the best for making canoes, and during the winter months, men worked at shaping war canoes, whaling canoes and other smaller craft.

Kee'hin, as the centre of Huu-ay-aht culture, was the largest of the villages and among the oldest. Here, generations of chiefs were born; they were the head chiefs of the tribe, and their exploits are preserved in Huu-ay-aht song and stories.

The title of chief was and still is inherited through the male line, from father to eldest son. The honorific name for head chief changed through the life of the chief. As a young chief, he may have been known as Nanolinal, and as he aged and organized his territorial rights, he became Tliishin. Many of the accounts of Huu-ay-aht history refer to Chief Tliishin, who was, undoubtedly, not always the same man.

In the centuries before contact with the outsiders, Kee'hin was the focus of power in southeastern Barkley Sound. And when the outsiders arrived, it was successive Chief Tliishins who welcomed these visitors into Huu-ay-aht territory. But by the end of the 19th century, Kee'hin was abandoned when people were drawn away by outside economic influences. They did not move far, just across the water to Cha'pis, at Dodger's Cove, Diana Island, where schooners and coasters could anchor.

Photographs of Kee'hin village taken in the early 20th century show how the forest had already begun to take it over. Only the uprights and ridgepoles of one house frame remain, but outside the house frame stand two six-metre-high welcome figures carved of cedar. Proud and weathered, these figures represent the first kuu-as, or Huu-ay-aht people, who came from the Sky spirit. The male figure's arms are outstretched in peace; one hand gestures the visitor to come, while a pointed finger on the other hand reminds the visitor to respect Huu-ay-aht laws. The female figure originally carried a cylinder in her hands that represents the topati, or inherited rights of the chief. Today these figures—once outside the house in which Chief Louie was born—are no longer at Kee'hin but on exhibition at the Royal BC Museum in Victoria. Modern versions of the figures now adorn the entrance to the House of Huu-ay-aht at Anacla, inviting and welcoming all who enter.

With a little imagination and the knowledge of past events, it is easy to visualize massive cedar-plank houses—10 or so in number, measuring from 10 by 15 metres to 25 by 12 metres in floor size and rising to 4 metres in height—set along the platform above the broad and curving beach. Upon this beach, dozens of whaling canoes and smaller canoes are drawn up to the high water through a series of channels cleared amid the stones and gravel to make canoe runs. Smoke from the village fires swirls at the interface of the cleared bush and forest. Dogs bark, children cry out and voices mix with the regular draw of the waves along the shingle and sand of the beach, in and out, in and out.

The headland provides excellent visibility out to the ocean and the entrance to Barkley Sound, across to the Deer Group Islands and up Trevor Channel, and it protected the village on the leeward side. Over the centuries, this unique geography led to conflicts between the Huu-ay-aht and other First Nations who coveted the spot. Many wars were fought and lives lost in its defence. Invaders inevitably came by ocean, so watchmen stationed on the headland had an important responsibility.

Cedar welcome figures representing Huu-ay-aht first ancestors at Kee'hin village, circa 1910. ROYAL BC MUSEUM, BC ARCHIVES PN4659

But the significance of Kee'hin runs deeper than this recent past. Many of the early accounts of the time when Huu-ay-aht ancestors still moved between the animal and human worlds happened at Kee'hin. The escapades of hero adventurers such as Eut'le'ten, a boy with magical powers who was born from tears, all connect with this place. Through the generations, elders told these stories to the young people, who then passed them on to their children. Some themes remind us, as outsiders, of stories we were told as children. Might common heroic stories told across cultures and continents signal a shared past?

The legend of a wild woman of the woods is known in various versions among different Vancouver Island First Nations. Her visage is recreated in oversized carved and painted cedar masks, worn by dancers who move and twirl around the fire centred in the traditional big house. In this flickering firelight, she is a frightening sight. The following Huu-ay-aht story is but one chapter in a series of supernatural adventures involving the hero Eut'le'ten—the boy who slays the wild woman.

The Wild Woman of the Woods

Danger lurked deep in the forest. Mothers cautioned their children to stay together and not to tarry when they collected firewood, for a wild woman lived in the forest. Her name was E'ish'so'oolth. She was so tall that when she walked through the forest her head brushed the lower branches of the great fir trees. E'ish'so'oolth was a Cheeha—a supernatural creature. Her lodge was hidden far inside the dark and canopied forest. It was made of cedar logs larger than anyone had ever seen before. E'ish'so'oolth would wait patiently, watching. Any girls and boys who wandered too far from their homes might come across this evil Cheeha, who would then capture them and take them to her lodge. And there, at her leisure, the children would be eaten, for the Cheeha was a cannibal.

E'ish'so'oolth was married to a giant Cheeha. He was

40

even taller and towered over his wife. His strength was greater than that of any man living on the coast. He was a brute with long matted hair that fell in tangles down around his great shoulders. His scowling face was filthy, and his eyes, sunken deep in his skull, glared out, sullen and angry. This Cheeha was not a being to trifle with. He could crush the life out of anything that displeased him.

Whenever people went missing, the Huu-ay-aht said that perhaps they had been captured by E'ish'so'oolth or her husband and taken to their lodge to be devoured. Naughty children were admonished to behave, "Be good or I will call E'ish'so'oolth!"

One day, some children from Kee'hin paddled a canoe out from their home and landed on a nearby shore, where they planned to gather seaweed. As they set out along the beach, each carried a woven cedar-bark container. Soon, one of the younger children became cold and tired, and he cried out to be taken home. The chores were not yet complete, so the others asked the boy to be patient, because they would leave for home shortly. But this child was not to be comforted and again he cried out. The others began to scold him and threatened to call E'ish'so'oolth. The threat had no effect, and the child continued to cry. In jest, one child made the mistake of teasing and called, "E'ish'so'oolth, E'ish'so'oolth, oh come E'ish'so'oolth."

The next moment a terrible being—tall and gaunt with stooping shoulders—stalked out from the forest. It was the Cheeha. She carried a mighty walking stick made of a gnarled tree branch. Waving this knotty stick in the air, she cried out, "Who called me by name?"

The children screamed and tried to run away, but as they scattered she laughed fiendishly, stretched out her walking stick and tripped them as they ran. The Cheeha then calmly caught them one by one with her lean hands. Using the sticky pitch from the fir tree, she sealed their eyes shut so that they would not be able to see which way they were going. She then threw the children into a basket on her back and started for home along a hidden track through the forest. But E'ish'so'oolth had to bend each time the path curved under the low and spreading branches of the fir trees, for she was so tall, and the basket on her back was now heavy. As she bent to go beneath these branches, four little hands popped up out of the basket top. Then, when a fir branch brushed the basket top, these little hands grabbed the branch tightly and held on fast. The Cheeha kept on going and did not miss the weight of just two children.

With their hearts thumping in their chests, the two children stayed as still as they could until they were certain E'ish'so'oolth had passed. They climbed down the tree limb and together they tried to free their eyes of the pitch. Once they could see a little bit, they ran for the beach, got in the canoe and headed for home. These lucky children told their mothers the terrible tale of how their playmates were scooped up and taken away. "By now surely they must be at the Cheeha's lodge. Perhaps they are already eaten," the children said.

Then came a sound as ancient as grief itself, as heart-breaking wails echoed through the village. Parents and grandparents, brothers and sisters, all mourned for the kidnapped children. The mothers sat, arms clasped around their knees, rocking back and forth. Steadily the power of their grief unleashed. They began singing the death lament. For these mothers there was no hope. No one had ever escaped from E'ish'so'oolth. Their children were gone, and there was absolutely no way to save them from their fate. For four days and nights the dismal song was heard. Weeks passed by and still they mourned. After a time, though, the healing began, and all but one mother drew comfort. She sat all alone, and each day at dawn, squatted on the sea grass along the shore, chanting the mourning song.

Early one morning, as she sat and cried, her tears flowed down and formed a little pool. This little pool of tears lay balanced among the grass blades. She did not notice it until, out of the corner of her eye, she caught a movement in the sand. The pool of tears was changing into something alive, something that—although very tiny—moved and wiggled. The mother picked up a mussel shell so that she could cradle the tiny form within it.

"What could this being be?" she wondered.

Gently she stood. Cupped in her hands lay the mussel shell

with its precious occupant. She carried it into her lodge and set it down in a safe and quiet place. The next day, within the shell lay a wonderful and tiny child. This child grew every day. The woman had to find larger and larger shells— oyster, mussel and clamshells—to form a cradle. She called this tiny being Eut'le'ten. He grew into a beautiful young boy. His limbs were well formed, his skin fair and his eyes clear and bright. This child was also wise beyond his years. For him, the most sorrowful thing was to hear his mother weeping, as she continued to do. Her constant pain gave him great sorrow, and one day he asked her, "Why do you weep so? Why do you chant the death lament?"

His mother looked at him with love in her eyes, yet sadness in her heart, and she told him about his sister and the tragedy that had befallen her. "E'ish'so'oolth came and took your sister, took her deep into the dark forest. I have no idea if she is alive or dead. I cannot live for the uncertainty and the pain."

"Do not weep, Mother. I will seek your daughter, who is my sister, and I will save her. Show me where she was last seen, and I shall search and find her."

Knowing that Eut'le'ten was a spirit child and could come to no harm, the woman gave him her blessing. But first she cautioned, "It is best to speak with the two children who escaped. Have them show you where your sister was taken from."

Armed with the children's information, Eut'le'ten

started out. When he arrived at the spot described by the two children, he broke through the dense salal that fringed the forest edge. He ducked into the thick woods, around the silvery spruce and the hemlock. As he followed the path, Eut'le'ten learned about the forest, for he was a newly born spirit child, and although invested with powers, had little knowledge of this place. He learned about salmonberry bushes, stinging nettles and devil's club, about mud and swamp, and about the difficulties of travelling in the bush. He saw black bears and other forest creatures and heard new and different bird calls.

The trail led him far inland. He travelled a great distance before he came upon a cool stream from which he quenched his thirst. As he stood alongside the water, Eut'le'ten saw the path broaden, and he carefully moved forward. There, in the clearing, was a lodge of such a size that he was dumbfounded. Surely this was the house of E'ish'so'oolth and her husband. But it was dusk, and he debated what to do. Perhaps it was best to wait until morning. If he rested, in the morning he could confront the Cheeha in the light. So Eut'le'ten climbed a tree that stood alongside the creek and went to sleep, drawing strength from the forest spirits. He prayed for courage and wisdom and strength to kill the Cheeha.

The next morning he awoke to sounds beneath him. Eut'le'ten looked down and saw E'ish'so'oolth coming to wash in the stream. She was a fierce and ugly creature.

Carefully he hid in the branches, confident she could not see him. But he was mistaken. As she leaned over an eddy in the stream to bathe, the water reflected the sky and trees, and he too was mirrored. In a flash she turned her eyes upward into the branches and saw Eut'le'ten partly concealed by the foliage. She smiled at him with a triumphant and expectant look, thinking what good fortune she had. Here was another child to capture.

She greeted him. "Good morning young friend, what brings you so far from your village? You must be cold and hungry. Why not come down from that tree and we can go to my lodge? It is nice and warm inside, for the fire is lit. I have some fresh berries which you are welcome to eat." Eut'le'ten wavered and did not answer right away, so she added, "I can hardly make you out, you are so well hidden in that tree. Come down so I can see you."

Confident that no harm could befall him, Eut'le'ten scampered down from the tree. E'ish'so'oolth looked at him and realized he was a truly beautiful child. He was perfect. Never before had she seen such a child.

"Why is your skin so fair?" she asked him.

Eut'le'ten answered, "When I was a boy, my mother laid me upon the ground with my head on a stone. Then my father placed a large rock on my forehead. This gave me the gift of fairness."

The Cheeha was very taken with the beauty of the young boy, and she thought about his words. "Would this work for me?" she wondered. "How much easier it would be to entice young children to my lodge if I was pleasant to look at. The children would not be so afraid if I was fairer."

Eut'le'ten read her mind, and before she had a chance to ask this selfish question herself, he answered it for her. "Would you like me to give you the gift of fairness?" he inquired. "Lie down on the stone here beside the creek. And then if you recline your head, I can place on your forehead a magic stone which will mould your features and make your skin fair."

E'ish'so'oolth determined to try at once and immediately stretched herself out on her back upon the flat rock. Then Eut'le'ten lifted a great rock and hurled it onto her head. He shouted, "Die E'ish'so'oolth, die! Never again will you steal children!"

But Eut'le'ten was not yet finished his task. The small boy then set out to search for E'ish'so'oolth's husband. It was not too difficult to locate this beast because loud pounding noises gave away his location. Eut'le'ten found the Cheeha at work splitting a fallen tree, using wedges formed from the western yew, the hardest of woods. With mighty blows of his stone hammer, he sunk a wedge deep into the log, splitting it open. This Cheeha was enormous and ugly. Although Eut'le'ten was prepared, he took a moment to gather his courage and watched as the huge man worked. Thunderous blow after blow fell upon the wedge, sinking it deeper into the log. The Cheeha's aim was true. The split grew wider and the sides of the rent pressed upon the wedge, so hard that if the wedge were dealt a glancing blow, it would fly out. As he hammered, the Cheeha saw a furtive movement out of the corner of his eye. He could feel someone watching him, someone who hid in the bushes.

"No one has any business spying on me," he thought. The Cheeha grew angry, but he managed to control himself. "It would be easier to kill this intruder by coaxing him to me than by frightening him off and chasing."

Cautiously, Eut'le'ten approached the Cheeha, moving slowly but deliberately so the giant would not realize that he was frightened. But that only angered the Cheeha, who expected fear from everyone who encountered him. The two looked long and hard at each other. The Cheeha conceived a plan. Taking his stone hammer, he struck another blow, pretending to hit the wedge, then letting the hammer drop deep in the crack and out of reach.

"Come here boy, I need your help. I have lost my hammer within this mighty tree. I cannot reach it, but you are smaller. Please jump in and get it for me, as I need it back."

The boy climbed up on the great log and then dropped down into the split, just as the Cheeha had requested. The Cheeha gave the wedge a sudden tap and it shot out. With a mighty snap, the sides of the great log came together like the mouth of a sea monster.

"Ha, ha!" cried the Cheeha, confident that he had killed Eut'le'ten in a single motion. But suddenly he saw a remarkable thing on the ground before him. A little pool of water formed, and from it there came an unearthly sound. As the Cheeha watched, the water moved and took shape, and the boy rose up. Nothing could harm this boy who could change his shape when in danger. He could transform into a primal pool of tears and then back again into his human shape. Astonished but resourceful, the Cheeha covered up for his actions.

"Oh, young boy," he said, "what a miracle. I thought for a moment that you had been crushed within the log. It was my mistake, and what a dreadful mistake it was. But how, tell me how, did you survive this accident? I saw with my own eyes that the log closed tight around you. And then in the next second you disappeared . . . and then . . . from a puddle of water you reappeared. Tell me, how did you gain this supernatural power?"

"It is a power that can be shared," claimed Eut'le'ten. "Come, I will teach you the way. If we try it just once, you will learn how to transform as well."

The Cheeha, like his wife, was weakened by selfishness. He wanted this power for himself. Quickly he reset the yew wedge deep into the heart of the log, opening up a split large enough for him to squeeze into. He carefully slid into the space. It was tight, tighter than he had envisioned.

"Are you ready?" called the boy.

"Yes!" roared the Cheeha, shaking the trees with his enthusiasm.

"Then die!" responded Eut'le'ten, and he took the hammer up and struck the side of the yew wedge. Out sprung the wedge and the sides snapped together, crushing the Cheeha, who shouted wildly in pain. Eut'le'ten ignored the Cheeha, whose bones were soon crushed to powder.

Eut'le'ten sped off to the great lodge and entered into it. It was gloomy because the light only entered through the doorway and the smoke hole. For some time, Eut'le'ten was unable to see anything, but gradually his eyes adjusted to the greyness and he made out the shapes of the baskets and other objects in the lodge. In the centre of the room was a smouldering fire, and in the hot ashes lay some heated stones. Beside the fire was a wooden box filled with water, ready to receive the heated stones, which would boil the water. Eut'le'ten's heart was heavy. He moaned. Was he too late to save the children? Had they already met their fate? Then he heard a sound that seemed to come from the far side of the lodge. Turning around, he saw some children imprisoned in basketry.

"Be brave, children," he said. "I am here to rescue you and return you to your homes. My name is Eut'le'ten and I am from your village. E'ish'so'oolth and her husband are both dead, so you have nothing to fear. There is no more danger."

But the children remained frightened. His voice was not familiar to them, and for all they knew, it could be a trick. Eut'le'ten then realized what part of the problem was. The children could not see. Speaking softly, he took a little whale oil and gently wiped their eyelids to remove the pitch that E'ish'so'oolth had used to close them so long ago. Able to see, the children's confidence increased. They looked into Eut'le'ten's eyes and saw that he spoke the truth.

"The Cheeha is really dead?" they asked him.

"Yes, and her husband too. Let's go home now."

Out of the lodge they ran, away from the dark and into the sunlit woods, along the path and eventually out into the bay. There was much rejoicing when Eut'le'ten returned with the children. Gently he led his sister to his mother, and the two were reunited. Now his mother wept with tears of joy.

CHAPTER

4

West Coast Peoples

THE NUU-CHAH-NULTH FIRST NATIONS on the West Coast lived in local groups that were parts of tribes. Although their language had a common base, dialect and words varied from tribe to tribe. Thus, the Huu-ay-aht tribe in Barkley Sound pronounce certain words or phrases differently from the Mowachaht in Nootka Sound or the Ahousaht in Clayoquot Sound. The Huu-ay-aht shared Barkley Sound with other tribes, including the Toquaht, the Tseshaht, the Ucluelet, the Uchucklesaht and the Hupacasath. Each tribe with its local groups claimed territories. Rights to harvest specific foods from both the ocean and the land were fixed to specific geographical areas, and these areas, or hahooth-lees, were owned by chiefs within each local group. These hahoothlees have been handed down in families through the generations and are acknowledged and known today. Likewise, the position of chief is hereditary and passes through the male line from father to eldest son.

Within the Huu-ay-aht tribe, there are four local groups that have been historically long-lived. These groups were basically independent of each other but had close ceremonial and military relationships. Each local group claimed a different geographical area within southeastern Barkley Sound. These groups were the Huu-ay-aht, the Kee'hinath, the Ch'ima'tokoso'ath and the Anacla'ath.

In the days before the outsiders came, the tribes in Barkley Sound jostled for rights to territories and resources. Tribes whose villages lay amid the rocky shores of the outside edges of the sound had to negotiate with other tribes in order to access their rich salmon rivers. Those rivers especially coveted were the Somass River at the head of Alberni Inlet; the Sarita River on the southern shores of the sound; and the Henderson and Nahmint River to the north. All species of salmon were eaten by coastal peoples, but for those who lived on the outside of the sound, access to the dog salmon was especially necessary; when smoked, dog salmon keeps longest without spoiling.

Those tribes living on the inside areas of the sound and with access to salmon streams then negotiated with those on the outside edges for the rights to hunt sea mammals on the open ocean, and for drift whale rights. Drift whales are whale carcasses that float along in the tide, eventually beaching or sinking. They represented a relatively easy way to gain the meat and oil of the whale, but the opportunities for whales to drift past the outside tribes to the inside tribes were relatively slim, hence the need for negotiations.

Seldom are people satisfied with what they hold, often coveting what is a neighbour's right. In the absence of rights or alliances, groups would sometimes take a strategic or resource-rich area by force. For the Nuu-chah-nulth First Nations, the balance of power shifted depending upon the strengths of particular tribes and upon the success of alliances and marriages. Politics in Barkley Sound were rarely stable, and warfare was often inevitable.

At times, a local group would be weakened by illness, scarcity of food or calamity and would have to make an alliance with another group for survival. Some tribes grew strong and thrived, developing aspirations to extend their territories in order to claim salmon-spawning rivers, herring bays or defensive sites. War was one way to do this. Intermarriage between local groups, and at times between tribes, was another way that authority and jurisdiction over land shifted as alliances formed. Marriages between high-ranking individuals mingled the blood of both tribes. Affiliations and families thus mixed.

But sometimes events conspired to try the alliances confirmed through marriages. One of the outside alliances made by the Huu-ay-aht was with a people who lived at

Clallam Bay on the southern shores of the Strait of Juan de Fuca, on the Olympic Peninsula, in what is now the United States. These Clallam people (unlike their Makah neighbours) were not Nuu-chah-nulth–speaking peoples, but Coast Salish, with distinct language and customs. Despite these differences, the Clallam and the Huu-ay-aht forged economic and political links through arranged marriages as a means of attaining security and good connections.

However, as in marriage, harmony is not always possible. Sometimes blame is cast for things done or not done, for insults, for slights intended or not intended. The Huu-ay-aht relations with the Clallam could be stormy. The following story recounts a devastating act of retribution taken against the Huu-ay-aht for perceived or actual wrongs done to Clallam or Clallam-descended people within the Huu-ay-aht community. Chief Louie, who presented this information within the context of two separate stories, estimated that the events occurred about 200 years earlier, some eight generations before he told of them.

Further details of the actual assault on Kee'hin came from another source. In 1922, three Huu-ay-aht elders—Sa'sawatin, his wife Yima'uk, and Hyna'um—sat on a sunny beach at Dodger's Cove. Alfred Carmichael paddled over from his campsite on Brady's Beach to meet them, for he had asked them to talk about the old days at Kee'hin. Hyna'um had lived at Kee'hin as a young boy. Carmichael brought a roughsketch map he had made of the remaining

Huu-ay-aht elders Sa'sawatin and his wife, Yima'uk.
ROYAL BC MUSEUM, BC ARCHIVES I-61566

house frames in the village, and Hyna'um told him the names of the heads of each family who had lived in the houses.

Carmichael left an important description of this day and how the elders spoke with him. There was no tape recorder, but the mood of the afternoon is captured in his words: "Old Sa'sawatin started the narrative, then Hyna'um would follow, and old Yima'uk would nod her head approvingly and say 'Ach, Ach, Yes, Yes,' and perhaps chip in with a bit of information . . . and in the telling their faces lighted up with eagerness. For hours they talked and I questioned."

The Clallam and Nitinat Attack Kee'hin

Tliishin was chief of the Huu-ay-aht and an extremely powerful man. He lived in the largest house at Kee'hin. At the time of the war, his hahoothlee—the rights and privileges he commanded over the territory—extended over a huge area. According to Chief Louie, Tliishin's hahoothlee stretched from the waterfall at Tsusiat River on the coast east of Cape Beale, all the way to Yashitko'a (Coleman Creek) on lower Alberni Canal. It was a vast territory.

This chief was married to a Clallam woman. It is not recorded if Tliishin had a voice in the choice of his marriage partner, but it is more likely that as a high-ranking person, it was his duty to strengthen his people through an alliance with another tribe. By allying with the Clallam, Tliishin was doing his chiefly duty.

The couple had twin daughters and two sons. It was the second son who caused the troubles. His name was Nasismis, which means "Carrying-Day-on-Beach." He was short-tempered and always fighting. He provoked others and behaved badly toward the women. In games of chance he cheated, and in games of strength he broke the rules. He was very devious. As a second son, he also was jealous of his older brother.

One day, Nasismis killed his older brother. He cut off his head in the way of the Clallam warriors and then hid the body. Upon returning to his village, Nasismis claimed he was puzzled.

"It was the strangest thing," he told his father. "My brother travelled with me, but then, as I faced out towards the ocean watching the gulls circling at something floating in the water beyond the point, I turned to make some comment, but he was not there. I just saw the last of him as he strode into the forest. I assumed he was trailing a deer and that he would soon return. I was patient, but there came no sight of him. I waited as the sun came close to the horizon and then went to the spot where I last saw him. I called and waited some more, but he did not return."

The story did not sit well with the young men of the village who did not like Nasismis, knowing him to be a liar. The next day they set forth with Nasismis, who showed them where he had last seen his elder brother. Indeed, nothing was to be found and there were no clues. But still the young men persevered and searched at the opposite beach. After a time, the body was discovered. Nasismis was blamed for the murder.

The young men spoke together, for they were very worried. With the eldest son dead, this wicked younger son was next in line to become their chief. It was not right that a man who would someday have much authority could kill his own brother; this was a frightening situation. The young men therefore resolved that they had no choice: they would have to kill Nasismis to prevent future troubles. And so as a group, the young men took Nasismis to a beach and killed him. It was a dangerously bold move to kill a future chief. But in their view there was no alternative. The consequences of this action, however, would prove devastating to the Huu-ay-aht people.

The mother of Nasismis was heartbroken, for she had lost both her sons. She was not convinced that her eldest son had died at the hands of his brother. She blamed both murders on the young men of the village. As soon as she was able, she went home to Clallam Bay to tell her people of the deaths. In the spring she returned.

Six months later, in August, word came to the Huu-ay-aht that their southern neighbours, the Nitinat, were planning war on them, and that these Nitinat people had asked the Clallam, Port Angeles and Lapush peoples to join them. The Huu-ay-aht prepared for war. Each day, the men washed themselves in the cold ocean water and scrubbed their bodies with hemlock until the blood flowed—this made them strong.

Under the cover of darkness, a huge raiding party paddled northward following the western coastline of Vancouver Island to enter Barkley Sound. The raiding party numbered 1,500 warriors. It had been a long and dangerous journey for the southern tribes who had joined the Nitinat, for they had come across the Strait of Juan de Fuca and the open ocean, far from their territory.

But they were motivated by an important point of honour. They had to take revenge for the deaths of the two brothers who were half Clallam and had been killed by the Huu-ay-aht. As sons of a high-ranking Clallam woman, these murdered brothers also had rank. Their murders cancelled out any marriage alliances between these two tribes. The Clallam raiders came to Kee'hin to kill Chief Tliishin, for he alone, as the highest-ranking person, would be sufficient compensation.

Fifty canoes rounded the point from Cape Beale, set to attack three Huu-ay-aht villages, at Ots'o'a, at Nanaskiyis (Brady's Beach) and at Kee'hin. As the warriors approached the promontory at Kee'hin, their paddle strokes became silent and there was no talk. The warriors had to be cautious. They knew that watchmen generally kept an eye out from behind stone walls high up along the cliff edge, some 30 metres above their canoes. But they detected no fires and no movement, only stone walls and silence.

Safely rounding the fortress rock, the canoes glided in on the waves to the beach on the lee side. It was then that the alarm went out. The invaders had been detected. With fierce battle cries, the Clallam warriors ran up the beach and along the footpaths onto the bench of land where the great houses stood. The fighting began. Stone clubs were swung beneath the night sky. In the initial confusion, some of the villagers managed to escape from the rear of the houses. These people then ran to a trail behind the fourth house, the house of Chief Tliishin. Up the path they sprinted in a desperate bid to outrace the enemy and reach their fort on the headland.

The chief and his family were among those who escaped.

As they neared the top of the path, each had to duck beneath a great, heavy log placed across the trail. This was just one of several obstacles set in readiness, for at the last moment, as the invaders crested the trail, the log would be released to roll and smash down upon them. The site of the fortress had been chosen well, for it was impregnable from the ocean side and only accessible from one route. At the top, the villagers hid behind metre-high defensive walls of earth and stone. From this protected vantage, they threw rocks from a stockpile down upon their assailants.

The fortress included small lodges as additional protection. One lodge also hid an escape route. It was into this lodge that Chief Tliishin and his family members fled. Inside, it was adrenaline and confusion. The lodge was dark; no fire burned. Babies cried and young children hid their heads under their mothers' arms. The young men bristled at being cooped up inside, away from the action. But they were responsible for Tliishin's safety. Far in the back, in the darkest corner of the lodge, panicked hands hurried to move the cedar cooking vessels, the feast bowls and the cooking utensils. Beneath these was a large, flat cedar slab. Scrabbling with their fingers, the men pried up the slab to reveal a hole that led down through the dirt, to a crevice in the rock below. By wiggling, a full-grown adult could fit through this crevice into a shaft that opened up into a cave. The cave was underground but above the sea level— a perfect hiding spot, but a spot that could shelter only a small portion of Tliishin's extended family. As quickly as they could, Tliishin and many of the youngest family members squeezed down the hole. Those remaining in the lodge replaced the cedar plank and the cooking vessels. They then prepared to hold off the enemy.

Even those Huu-ay-aht who managed to make their way up the trail to the fortress never stood much of a chance. By their sheer numbers, the Clallam overpowered the Huu-ay-aht and were victorious. After four days, the battle sounds and the cries of the wounded were heard no more by those hidden deep in the rock of Kee'hin. But Tliishin and the young men and women remained in the cave, not daring to venture forth. Finally the Clallam departed. Although Chief Tliishin had escaped, the Clallam were satisfied because in destroying the entire village, the honour of the Clallam mother had been upheld.

Tliishin and the fortunate group of young people emerged from the cave to find their village burned and destroyed, and all their families clubbed to death and beheaded. They could not stay there, for they did not know what further plans the Clallam might be formulating. And if not the Clallam, soon their neighbours would hear about the slaughter and come to take over the Huu-ay-aht territory.

Hidden in the brush near the shore, they found a canoe that had escaped Clallam eyes. To preserve their people, the survivors resolved to seek haven from the Clallam and from others who might harm them. They paddled along the shores of Barkley Sound to their salmon-rich main river. This river, later called the Sarita by outsiders, was to be their refuge. They paddled the canoe up the river, heading deep into the forest and away from the coast. There they would be safe.

The news of Kee'hin's destruction spread quickly. Anticipating further attacks, many of the Huu-ay-aht in the surrounding small villages fled to the larger villages at Ots'o'a and Nanaskiyis. These villages were more secure because they had defensive sites adjacent to them. There were many people now camped together. But, as at Kee'hin, they were caught unaware by the approaching warriors. The war canoes came silently onto the beach. Those who survived the first wave of attack retreated to the fortresses. Despite valiant defence, the villages were overrun.

In desperation, parents at the two villages put their children and young adults into whaling canoes, and they paddled away to hide. Travelling independently of Tliishin and his group, these youngsters also made their way up Barkley Sound to the Sarita River, which had in the past afforded protection. They travelled silently, ever alert for their enemies. The first group, the Kee'hin survivors, had headed for Keekee'hinkook, on the south branch of the Sarita. The other villagers, who followed within days of the Kee'hin survivors, went a different route; they stayed on the main branch of the river, paddling and pulling the canoes up its entire length until they reached Sarita Lake. From there they paddled to Wihata, a refuge site that would serve them well.

These survivors took many precautions. Through the years they took great care to keep their location a secret, for they were small in number and vulnerable. For 19 years they remained hidden. They multiplied and became strong, anticipating the time when they could return to the coast and reclaim their territories. But neither group knew of the other's existence, so well were they hidden. Each group assumed that they were the only survivors, and each mourned for the other.

None of their neighbours knew that these Huu-ay-aht had survived, either. All the tribes knew was that Kee'hin, Nanaskiyis and Ots'o'a all lay in ruins and that their people had disappeared. As the years passed, other First Nations moved into Huu-ay-aht territories, those territories that were once Tliishin's domain. These interlopers took over some of the old village sites, hunted on Huu-ay-aht land, fished in their salmon streams and took the drift whales in their waters. At the mouth of the Sarita River, where the land is flat and the beach is wide, Hach'a'ath and Tseshaht people moved in and established a village. They built it on the very land that the Huu-ay-aht used in salmon season, a land they called Numukamis.

During a chance encounter one day in the forest, high above the river, Huu-ay-aht hunters from the hidden villages unexpectedly met. One group came upon an elk that was acting suspiciously; it seemed curiously weakened. They shot at the elk with an arrow, and it died. As the hunters squatted around the carcass preparing to butcher it, they saw that the elk had another wound from an arrow, but it was not one of their arrows. This was the reason the elk was weakened. Wondering what the presence of this strange arrow could mean, they suddenly heard conversation in the forest. The conversation was between people they did not recognize, but who spoke their language.

Tentatively they called out, "Who are you?"

The reply came back. "We are Huu-ay-aht people. We have taken refuge in this place. Who are you?"

It soon became evident that the hunters were facing other Huu-ay-aht people who they had assumed to be dead. Each group had hidden so well that they believed they were all alone in the upper Sarita territory. How odd to face those who had been thought long gone! The groups had mourned for each other, and for their Chief Tliishin, but now, with this chance discovery, the mourning could end. The chiefs and elders in each group met for the first time in many years. There was great rejoicing. For Tliishin, it was a time of special significance. He was now much older and had worried about the fate of his people, but now, joined together as one, they gained strength in their numbers.

Speaking among themselves, the elders resolved to prepare the people to reclaim their territories. Henceforth, they planned together. The young men learned the art of war from these elders, who taught them as they once had been taught. It was a time of intense mental and physical preparation.

But meanwhile, as the training continued, another chance discovery set in motion a timeline for the Huu-ay-aht revenge. At the mouth of the Sarita, at the place called Numukamis, the Hach'a'ath and Tseshaht interlopers had a quandary. For several days in a row now, mysterious objects had been floating down the river. Some were discovered at the beach and some were spotted on the rocks and back eddies at the river mouth. These objects were none other than grass-formed dummies in the shape of fish—the sort used by young men when they practised spearing salmon. Some of the dummies even had spearheads caught in them. With trepidation, the Hach'a'ath villagers picked up the objects and brought them to their elders. What could they mean?

"It is apparent," the elders said, "that unbeknownst to us, people must live upriver. They must be very confident people to have given away their presence by allowing these practice fish to float away." The elders then began to debate. What should their actions be? That night, a man named Kwaxswiqol, a slave who many years ago had been taken captive from his Huu-ay-aht village, whispered to his wife. "I must go upriver and see. If there are people living up there, they may be my people, the people who survived the raids. I will go to see if by any chance my chiefs are alive. They will not kill me if they are my chiefs. Don't you tell any of those who live with us in this house. I will return."

He left at high tide that night, paddled upstream and then poled and dragged the canoe up the river until he reached a beach just below Tl'itsnit. There, panting in the dark, he could smell the smoke from their fires. Frightened, he still continued on, determined to learn whether his kinsmen lived.

Kwaxswiqol called out to the villagers. The men on the security watch heard him and understood his words. They took him before the 10 chiefs, some of whom were elders and could recall the old days. They believed his story. Then they questioned him and, upon learning details concerning the village below, resolved to make a pre-emptive strike. The plan was that Kwaxswiqol should return to the village. At daybreak the next morning, he and his family would climb up and sit on the roof of their house and sing a tse'yka, a sacred song. This would be the signal to attack. With the family up on the roof, they would be safe and away from the battle.

At sunrise, Kwaxswiqol and his family moved to the roof and began to sing. The world seemed very still, until all at once from the forest came the war cries and frightening sounds of the attackers, who came in hard with their stone clubs. In the village of 80 people, there was bloodshed. Soon the Huu-ay-aht warriors gathered the few surviving Hach'a'ath and sent them back to where they had come from to spread the word. The Huu-ay-aht were mighty once again and now reasserted claim to all their territories.

Power Shifts

During their long history, the Huu-ay-aht have had periods when they were weakened and vulnerable to raids from neighbouring tribes, and also times when they were strong in number and could make overtures against their neighbours or reclaim lands previously taken from them. One of the more renowned stories is a saga of war and revenge between the Huu-ay-aht and the Ucluelet, who fought for jurisdiction over Barkley Sound during the 19th century.

This war, which became known as "The Long War," lasted many generations. Finally, after years of fighting within Barkley Sound, a Huu-ay-aht chief, whose name was Nanolinal, grew tired. He had witnessed a 10-year-long series of raids between his people and the Ucluelet and Hach'a'ath. All that had been accomplished were the deaths of many young men, which meant that it was harder for those remaining to hunt for food and survive each year. But still the raids continued, and Nanolinal believed that unless there was a way to end the battles for once and always, all that would be accomplished would be the continued weakening of his people.

"Why are we doing this?" he asked his people. "Why are we fighting all the time? At times many of us are killed. They killed my father. Our country is always in danger. We should work out some way in our method of fighting so that we may kill our enemy once and for all, and get back to a peaceful time." But no one had any idea how they could do this. No one, that is, except Nanolinal. He had a bold scheme.

"Let us go to the Sarita River," he said to the people. So 50 young men went to the Sarita River, and there they killed an elk for its skin to make coats and hats. Then they killed a black bear. They lined the coats and hats with bear bones. Soon they were all equipped with elk-skin coats and elk-skin hats lined with black bear bones. Spears and arrows would not penetrate the coats, and their heads would not be broken if hit with a war club. It took three months for all these preparations, which included fasting. Nanolinal believed that overeating made the people weak, so they learned not to eat so much as a preparation for war.

In July they were ready and went on a war raid. They wore masks and their elk clothing. Fifty warriors paddled away in canoes, with each canoe holding up to 12 men. They travelled swiftly, with the element of surprise, to Effingham Inlet, home of the Hach'a'ath. Leaving the canoes on the beach, the warriors approached the village through the trees. They emerged from the forest, clubbing and killing. They set fire to the villages and achieved almost total destruction. Not a single Huu-ay-aht warrior was killed or injured. The raid was a complete success, due almost entirely to the protective armour, which had given the Huu-ay-aht great confidence. The victors set off for home, returning to Sarita, where they settled.

Soon, news of their prowess spread, and the Huu-ay-aht grew strong. The neighbouring Nitinat and the Uchucklesaht also banded with them to assist in pushing back their common enemies. The Ucluelet and others from across the sound were almost decimated. Another decade went by. Although the Huu-ay-aht were successful and won many battles, they were frequently fighting, which played havoc with the seasonal round of food gathering. How can you focus on hunting a whale when you are preparing for battle? How can you let your guard down long enough to move with your family to the salmon stream when it is time to catch sockeye? The constant stress made relaxing impossible and life tense for years. There was no peace anywhere. Finally, a Ucluelet woman, a chief, appeared off the Huu-ay-ahts' shores. She came to ask that they stop the warring. Nanolinal listened and thought, "This is good; this chief is wise. She has spoken the very thoughts I have had myself."

The Huu-ay-aht agreed to stop the war and to keep peace in the sound. From that time on, they would, at intervals, gather with the Ucluelet to eat together, to share salmon at the Sarita River and to sing songs and tell stories. There would be no more war.

The peace survives to this day.

5

Two Villages and their People Disappear

TODAY, WE ARE WELL AWARE that seismic events occur on a regular basis in the Pacific Northwest area. Movement in the plates that make up the earth's crust causes earthquakes. When two plates slide past each other or one moves over another, they create shock waves that ripple through the rock, shaking the earth's surface. Two such plates lie off the shores of the Pacific coast and move regularly, resulting in some 200 earthquakes recorded by scientists each year. Most of these quakes are small and often not noticed by the average person, but in the recent past, there have been several earthquakes of a magnitude sufficient to cause damage to a built environment and to initiate movement of the ocean water. In 1963, a quake measuring 8.6 on the

Richter scale occurred off the coast of Alaska. This quake triggered a huge tsunami, a wave that grew in intensity as it travelled across the ocean. When the tsunami reached Vancouver Island, it surged up Alberni Inlet and spewed onto the land and the town of Port Alberni, causing massive destruction.

Archaeological excavations on the Pacific coast show evidence of disruption in the occupation of First Nations resource sites and villages, and of profound geological upheaval. This information, combined with geophysical data gathered by scientists studying the earth's features, clearly indicates that in the centuries prior to contact with the outsider society, other significant earthquakes likely occurred, including a cataclysmic event that took place just over 300 years ago. Scientists agree that the evidence indicates a massive tsunami, some 10 to 15 metres in height, rolled across the Pacific Ocean and smashed into the shoreline along the outer coastal areas.

In Japan, on the opposite side of the Pacific Ocean, a tsunami struck at the same time. Japanese survivors recorded the event as occurring in the year 1700. Based on the archaeological and geophysical evidence, the tsunami was triggered by a quake in the magnitude of a plus 9. If the quake originated somewhere in the middle of the Pacific Ocean, it would have triggered waves radiating outwards, which would have rolled together, building in intensity until they hit land in both Japan and North America with devastating consequences. This is the earthquake that triggered the huge wave recounted in the stories of First Nations, told over generations and recounted to others in the years since. The quake and tsunami changed life in the Huu-ay-aht world in a very dramatic way.

Once again, Chief Louie is the source for the following story. This account, unlike some of the other stories he told, is very brief. He was passing on just the barest of information because that was all that existed. Only a few people survived the tsunami. Some additional details have been woven into this version to flesh out the rather terse recitation and to put the event in geographical context.

Annihilation

This is a story about the people who lived at Pachena Bay and the Luh'taa people. A great chief of the people living at Kee'hin had four sons, and he decided that it was time for them to marry. He sent his sons in a grand canoe procession south along the coast to their neighbours who lived at the village of Luh'taa, located beyond Pachena Bay. These neighbours were great whalers and had the best of two worlds: ready access to whales offshore and an excellent vantage point to spot drift whales. Further up the coast, they owned the Pachena River, a good source for salmon in the autumn.

It was not a difficult journey for the sons; once the canoes rounded the rocky cliffs of Cape Beale, the voyage could be accomplished within a day. The people at Luh'taa could see the canoes in the distance as they approached. The canoes did not carry warriors painted for battle; rather, the chief's sons and their supporters wore ceremonial regalia proclaiming their family privileges.

As the canoes approached the village, young men came out to greet them and helped pull the canoes onto the beach. The chief's house—the largest in the village—was clearly visible to the Kee'hin men, but as was the custom, they remained on the beach to begin the marriage ceremony. It was to last four days. They sat on the beach and made overtures to the chief, whose name was Hayoqwis'is, which means "Ten-on-Head-on-Beach." Chief Hayoqwis'is received his name because of his whaling abilities, having beached 10 humpback whales at a single time.

As the highest-ranking person, Hayoqwis'is had authority over this village of Luh'taa and also over other villages at Anacla, at the mouth of Pachena River, at Malsit, located high on the edge of Pachena Bay, and at Mals'aas, just a little farther along the coast and also high atop a steep bank. Malsit was a good place to use as a base for halibut fishing. Chief Hayoqwis'is also claimed authority over the region south of Malsit, down to the territory controlled by the Nitinat people.

As the ceremony unfolded, the Kee'hin sons outlined to Hayoqwis'is their reason for visiting. "We wish to purchase a bride," the eldest son explained. "Our father has sent us to you to find a wife from among your daughters. It will be good for us both to have ties of kinship between our groups."

Hayoqwis'is replied, "Yes, I agree it would be a wise thing to do, to unite our houses in marriage. But you must understand, my daughter is very precious to me. Her happiness is also important. I want to know that the man she will marry is worthy of her, not just because of his birthright, but because he is a strong man, and capable of leading his people. I consent to give my daughter in marriage to the man who proves himself worthy enough."

Thus the chief outlined a series of topati, or tests of strength and endurance, which would prove who among the four sons was worthy of his daughter. One of the topati was a broad jump. To earn Hayoqwis'is's daughter, one had to successfully jump four fathoms (approximately eight meters). This contest took place on a rocky shore at Luh'taa. The sons of the Kee'hin chief took their turns. The younger brother was the first to make the jump, but as he landed, his face smashed against the cliff and he broke his head and died. Eventually, another brother succeeded, and by passing the topati, he earned the eldest daughter of the chief as his bride. The canoes left almost immediately for Kee'hin.

Sometime afterward, at night, while the people in Luh'taa slept, the earth began to shake. The houses on the sandy beach swayed and the cedar boards shifted. By the time the people awoke—if they awoke at all—it was chaos. Beneath them, the sand shifted and turned to liquid; all their houses flattened and fell into the sand. There was no time to get into the canoes, and no way to make the distance from their houses to the water, for now all was liquid. Canoes floated out to the ocean while the villagers slid beneath the sand. And soon, very soon, the tide that pulled back from the beach and released the canoes brought into the beach an enormous wave.

The wave, which must have glistened in the moonlight, crested and crashed as it hit the land, its power splintering the mighty fir and spruce trees in the forest well beyond the village site. As it sucked back with a tidal strength never before imagined, the wave took with it the forest, the animals, the rocks and the entire village. All were killed; none remained living among those who had gone to sleep that night in the village of Luh'taa.

On higher ground, in the village of Malsit, the houses were built upon rock, not sand. As the earth shook, these houses swayed and some of the cedar planks and ridgepoles fell, but that was all. When the tsunami came, the people of Malsit were not swept out to sea, for their village was higher than the wave. But this was a small village, with not many people in it. Some of the people were out whaling, and these people, the ones out on the ocean, were also lost.

Other Luh'taa'aht villages were swept away or damaged. All along the coast, people died. Those who survived woke to a world that would never be the same. Gone were many of their houses and canoes, much of their food, their grease, their smoked fish and their dried berries. It was terrible devastation. With the loss of the people came also a loss of history and the continuity of traditions.

Of the Luh'taa'aht nobility, only the eldest daughter of the chief, the one who had left by canoe, survived. She was now married to the son of a Kee'hin chief. As she was carried by canoe to her new home, she never dreamed that soon she alone would hold the rights and prerogatives of her father and her entire tribe. To the Kee'hin people she brought the territory extending from the Nitinat boundary up to Pachena Bay. Thus, the Kee'hin chief assumed control over a larger territory and over those few that survived at Malsit.

The devastation wrought that night in 1700 necessitated great change in the social structure of the Huu-ay-aht people. The losses of life, possessions and food sources stripped local groups of much of their effectiveness. There were significantly fewer people, and many were without homes or food. The villages no longer had security of numbers and had to make new alliances in order to survive. Previously independent people had to move from their now-isolated circumstances to be closer to others. This dramatic change in the social set-up was echoed throughout Barkley Sound.

Cape Beale Underworld

An earthquake—possibly the same one that triggered the tsunami that annihilated Luh'taa—wiped out the people living at Cape Beale. But the earthquake is just part of the story of Cape Beale's people. This story, which features a young whaling chief named Si'xpa'tskwin (meaning "Hunter-of-Humpback-Whales"), comes from Chief Louie.

It all began one day when Si'xpa'tskwin and three other young chiefs were out hunting. They followed a bear into its cave and then went far inside, beyond the opening. Deep within the cave it got lighter, and soon these four young chiefs found themselves in a wonderful land, a good country with a plentiful salmon river. They walked toward the river, and there killed many salmon, which they carried home in packs on their backs. These salmon were the type known as winter-springs.

Upon returning, the chiefs made sure that representatives from every house came to take a share of the salmon. In this way, they distributed their wonderful bounty evenly among the villagers. Around the fire that night, the young men told their remarkable story.

"A land beneath the earth? And one filled with salmon and forests?" asked the villagers. "Let's go and see for ourselves." So they nominated 10 young men to go to the cave the following day. These men, too, saw the good country, as well as amazing birds called Cheehayit'a. The 10 men walked around in this extraordinary land to get a better sense of it and then speared some salmon and returned home.

The next day, everybody at Cape Beale wanted to go to this marvellous place and to see for themselves how easily the salmon could be caught. It seemed like a dream come true. For the people at Cape Beale, living as they did on a rocky headland, access to salmon rivers was limited. They had negotiated an arrangement with another group to use a spot on the Sarita River to gather salmon, but this was only seasonal. The fact that they might have access to their own private, albeit underground salmon river was almost too good to be true.

Nearly every man lined up to see the cave. Those who were married went with their wives; many also took blankets and other items. Si'xpa'tskwin would not go this time, for something did not feel right, and he told his father so.

"Please father, do not go, it is not right to go. Listen to me please."

Neither Si'xpa'tskwin nor his father went, but most of the others did go. They walked inside the cave for days, eventually coming out at the Sarita River after having passed through the bowels of the earth—for the river they had followed was under the earth. It was there, in this river, that the winter-spring salmon spawned. The people decided that they would prefer living in a land with abundant salmon. The Sarita was not theirs, but this underground river was their own discovery, so they stayed beneath the ground. Some 200 people never returned to Cape Beale. Only a handful of young adults, the children and elders, along with Si'xpa'tskwin and his father, remained at the village.

After several days had passed, a few of the remaining

villagers decided that they would join the others at the magical country. "Surely it must be a perfect place, otherwise they would have returned by now. We'll go tomorrow."

But before they had time to pack up, the land began to shake. It was an earthquake that caused widespread destruction. It flattened the hillside, and a landslide of mud and rock poured over the opening to the cave and tunnel. There was now no way the remaining villagers could follow their family members and no way for the 200 people in the cave to return. These people became a ghost people, seen now and then only as apparitions. They were trapped underground and became wild.

Most of the young men had gone to the cave, and these were the whalers. Without their whaling chiefs and whaling crews, the villagers could not catch whales. They had to move and start afresh elsewhere. So they put what they owned into the big whaling canoes and paddled to the Sarita River. Next, they moved up the river to a place called Ferns-on-Beach, and there they set up a new village. From this spot they could fish for dog salmon, enough for their winter food.

But then Si'xpa'tskwin saw another black bear. Again he was out with three other young men, and again they followed the bear for a while, thinking it might lead them into its lair and that this would be profitable. They had their bows and arrows and were quite prepared. After a while, the bear headed up the Sarita, looked back and saw that it was being followed. But still it continued its lumbering gait, seeming not to care. A little farther on, though, the bear slowed, stooped down and entered into a hole.

Well, Si'xpa'tskwin and the others paused for a second—hadn't this already happened before, and with quite devastating consequences? But curiosity got the better of them and they followed the animal. Into the hole they crawled. It was dark, but even so, there was a steady breeze coming from farther within. The young men ventured far beyond the opening, and soon the hole became a tunnel that they could stand inside. Curious, and emboldened by the breeze, the men continued down the dark passage, convinced that soon they would come up elsewhere on the riverbank. For surely the breeze they felt on their skins meant an opening to the outside.

Down, down they walked, and then, startling them ahead in the dark, they saw the shining eyes of the bear. Suddenly they became very tired and lay down on the dry earth to sleep. Upon awakening, refreshed and energized, they continued on, again seeing the shining eyes of the bear in the distance down the tunnel. Eventually the breeze got stronger. Then, much to their surprise, they came out not on the riverbank near their new village, but in that same underground wonderful land. It seemed the tunnel was connected to the one they had followed from Cape Beale.

Amazingly, it was daylight within the bowels of the

earth, and the young men could see the abundant winter springs and the perfect land to live in. Excitedly they caught two salmon each and carried them on their backs, away from this place, back into the tunnel. They had to stop several times to sleep, for it was a longer distance back than they had realized on their journey in. It was dark and late by the time they reached home. Si'xpa'tskwin woke his father, and the others awoke their families. They stayed up all night, roasting the winter-spring salmon on sticks around the fire and talking about this new land. The idea, of course, was that if the underground land could be reached from this new cave, then the missing villagers could be found. Moreover, since the underground land was rich and plentiful, they could all go to live there. That way everyone would be reunited.

The next morning, every last villager resolved to go, including Si'xpa'tskwin, who this time convinced his father to go, too. Everyone gathered up their belongings. It took quite some time to pack and prepare. The only things not going to the underworld were the whaling canoes, which the villagers left on their sides on the beach. By nightfall, all had wiggled into the cave and set off underground.

Later, neighbours of the villagers came upon the whaling canoes and wondered why they lay abandoned on the beach. To their amazement, not a soul was in the village. But footprints led up and along the river's edge. As these neighbours followed the footprints, another large earth tremor occurred. The land shifted, and the trees swayed and cracked. It was frightening, but the neighbours persisted and followed the footsteps to where they ended, rather abruptly, at a spot on the river that was much changed. The land had given way, and now a waterfall lay where none had before. This is the place called Took'ool. And it was here that the opening to the underworld was sealed forever.

6

Whales and Whaling

"WHALES WEAR CLOTHES, LIKE PEOPLE, only the clothes they wear are skin and blubber and fins. They put these clothes on during the day, but at night, go back to their homes under the water and take these coats off. That is why whales are not often seen at night, and why the hunters have to be on the ocean by dawn when the whales first leave their houses and come to the ocean surface."

With this explanation, an elder might initiate discussions with children about the Huu-ay-aht world and about the place of animals within it. Whales were a significant part of human life because their bodies fed the tribes, their blubber and grease providing important nutrition.

Not all Huu-ay-aht people had the right to hunt whales.

It was a sacred privilege, inherited by certain men within certain families. A great whaler was often also a chief, so his status was doubly large. Success in whaling came not just with luck or with skill in harpooning, but through adequate spiritual preparation that focused the mind for the danger of the hunt and tuned it to the nuances of whale behaviour to get close to the whale without alarming it in any way. This ability was obtained through ritual purification and prayer, and by dedicating one's life to success in the hunt.

Whales are powerful and intelligent creatures. A whaler and his crew had to prepare themselves to be strong, both spiritually and physically, in order to be worthy of hunting the whale and to be successful at it. A whaler performed "oosimich," a purificatory bathing ritual. Oosimich was designed to toughen the physical body and to cleanse it of the human scent, as the warm, sweaty human body was disliked by the spirits. It was important not to anger the whale by being contaminated with unclean things that it could smell. So the whaler would go to his sacred spot and perform the bathing rituals. For four nights during the waxing of the moon, he bathed in cold fresh water and scrubbed his body with bundles of nettles and secret plants, sometimes including cedar bark. During each session, he prayed that the whale would come close alongside his canoe. Then for four nights during the waning of the moon, he bathed at a secluded spot at sea. He swam counterclockwise, moving slowly like a whale—floating, diving and blowing. Every four circuits he came out of the water to scrub his body with plants and to pray.

Whalers had specific whaling canoes that were shaped to fit the function. It was important that they be made well, so they would glide evenly through the water. Like the whalers, the canoes had to be purified and remain clean. Whaling canoes were never drawn up on the beach or dragged down to the water, because if they were, they would come in contact with human smells or touch rotting things on the sand. Instead, the canoes were carried down to the water on lifting poles.

Whaling canoes were made of red cedar. They measured 10 metres or more in length and could be 2 metres wide. Some of the best cedar was found near Kee'hin, but strong, tall, ancient cedar was plentiful throughout Huu-ay-aht territory. The process for making a canoe involved many steps, the first being selection of the best tree, ideally found near the edge of the forest or near enough to be hauled out on rollers. Canoes were carved out of the tree trunk, not constructed of planks or boards. Once the tree was selected, it had to be felled. In the days before the outsiders provided metal, trees were felled using tools of stone, bone and hardwood. Once a tree was on the ground, men removed the branches and bark. With the tree trunk clear, the canoe makers used wedges to help split the wood along the grain and shaped the hull first. The inside was dug and carved out next. Great care was spent getting the correct thickness in the

Whaling canoes and a busy beach at Cha'pis, 1902.
ROYAL BC MUSEUM, BC ARCHIVES PN6528-D

walls and floor of the canoe so that it would sit straight in the water and stay balanced when paddled by its crew of eight—a harpooner, a steersman and six paddlers.

Normally, the tree was felled in the autumn and the canoe was roughed out over the winter months and finished in the spring. Then the canoe had to be moved from where it lay on the forest floor. During this complex process, logs were propped beneath the canoe to lift and guide it as it was pushed along on wood rollers to the beach. There the canoe would be given its final shape—fine-adzed and sanded with dogfish skin, steamed to shape, and then the bow and stern scarfed on.

The whaling season began each April with the northward migration of the mah'ak, or California gray whales. Si'xpa'ox, or humpback whales, mostly came in the summer, as did eehtop (right whales) and kotsqu (sperm whales). After performing oosimich, the whaler would call together his crew, and they would set forth before dusk so they would be far from shore before the dawn. Sometimes a whale was sighted, signalling that a pod might be travelling through, but often, too, the whaler would dispatch the canoe on the basis of a prophetic dream.

It could take a long time to get close to the whales, as they were usually quite a distance from land. Once on the hunting grounds, it often took equally long to situate the canoe so that it would be in the best position for harpooning a whale. Ideally, the canoe would be on the left side of the whale as it breached on the surface of the ocean, and then the harpoon could be thrust just as the whale began to submerge with the flukes on the upswing. By positioning in this fashion, when the harpoon pierced the whale, the whale would react by swinging away from the canoe, not into it. This was a very dangerous operation. Whalers could not right an overturned canoe, and they were much too far away from land to survive the ocean temperatures. If successful in the kill, the whalers then needed to prevent the whale from sinking, and they faced a marathon operation to manoeuvre the carcass to land, ideally to the village beach.

Like all animals, whales have a life cycle. When they die, they do not sink right away. Instead, gases quickly form inside them, making their carcasses buoyant. They float, buffeted by the wind and tide, often for some time before they either rot and sink, or wash up upon the shore. A whale that has washed up onshore is called a hon'i, or drift whale. It might be found any time during the year and does not appear just by chance, but because a chief had been diligent in his oosimich.

The right to recover drift whales belonged to the chief who owned the hahoothlee, the ocean or beach area where the carcass was found, or to the man who owned the rights to drift whales, which could be separate from ownership of territory. Once ownership was established, a strict protocol had to be followed. This protocol dictated the division of the carcass. The chief received the first piece, the saddle of the back near the fin. Then the harpooner and the other chiefs each took their pieces of blubber. The crew of the whaling canoe, or the individuals who helped tow in the drift whale, then received their pieces. The remaining skin and blubber was divided up among the villagers according to rank. Delicacies such as the tongue, lower jaw, flippers and flukes were also distributed according to rank.

The two whaling stories included in this chapter come from a man whose name is recorded only as William. To date,

A dead whale awaiting butchering at Cha'pis, Diana Island, circa 1910. ROYAL BC MUSEUM, BC ARCHIVES PN16345

relatively little is known about him, except that he was born around 1870 and had both Huu-ay-aht and Tseshaht ancestry. In 1913 and 1914, William was one of several cultural advisors consulted by anthropologist Edward Sapir. Based on the number of histories and narratives he provided to Sapir, it is clear that William was very knowledgeable concerning many details of traditional life in Barkley Sound. His father, whose name was Haq'to'a, was half Huu-ay-aht, and it is from him that William learned Huu-ay-aht narratives.

A Whale and a Story

Chief Si'xpa'tskwin of Cape Beale was always trying to better himself as a whaler. He performed oosimich, he fasted and he prayed. One day, he determined that if he had better eyesight and could see far into the distance, he could lead his people to more whales. But how could he accomplish this? As he pondered the situation, he looked at all the other animals in his world. Many of them had very keen eyesight and because of this could protect themselves well. Others had great skill in locating food. He was most impressed by birds. He knew that the eagles and hawks were amazing hunters. From high in the sky they spotted their prey and then from these great distances swept down with deadly accuracy. Si'xpa'tskwin resolved that he would do what he could to improve his eyesight by borrowing the eyes of a bird. He took the eyes of an osprey and worked with them for many hours. Finally, he was successful in finding a way to alter and then combine them with his own eyes.

Now when Si'xpa'tskwin looked out over the water he could see far in the distance. He was most happy with his new eyes and spent the rest of the day looking out to sea, searching the horizon. He searched, of course, for whales. Looking south one day, Si'xpa'tskwin saw a drift whale way, way out. Without his new eyes he would never have had this power.

Several young men were sitting on the rocks on the

beach with Si'xpa'tskwin. He said to them, "Look, there on the horizon, there are many birds, seagulls, eating the whale."

The other men looked but did not see it. "Are you sure?" they questioned. "We can't see anything, and we don't really believe that you have the eyes of an osprey."

"Yes, the whale is there, and we should set our canoes in the water and tow the whale in to the village."

"But I don't know if it is worth it for the bother," one man said. "It is only your word that you can see this whale."

"Let's go and see it," another replied. And so they did. They lifted a big canoe down the beach, and 10 of the young men got into it. They began paddling. With so many paddlers, the canoe sprinted forward through the waves. On they paddled. Every now and then Si'xpa'tskwin would stand up and look ahead on the horizon, checking that they were on course. The young men paddled in the direction he told them, for they still could see nothing in the water.

"It's close now, it isn't far now," Si'xpa'tskwin said as they paddled, going farther and farther out to sea. Soon Cape Beale went down over the horizon. Now it was late afternoon, then it became evening. Finally, the young men could see something in the distance.

"Sure enough, there are many birds," said one of them.

Then they saw it, floating on the sea. It was indeed a dead whale. They manoeuvred the canoe close to the carcass. They were extremely tired and stopped paddling.

"You climb up onto it and cut off a chunk of blubber," they said to Si'xpa'tskwin. He climbed onto the whale and cut off a chunk. The young men looked at each other and then looked around. It was then that they realized the situation they were in. It was a long, long way to the shore. They could not even see the land, they were so far off it. Yes, Si'xpa'tskwin had amazing eyesight to have seen this drift whale, but what had he done bringing them out so far from home? How would they ever have the strength to drag the carcass to shore? Why had they kept paddling without thinking of the fix he was getting them into?

"There is no way that we can bring this whale home with us," one young man whispered to another. "We are far, too far out to sea and will die in the trying. I for one think we should just leave Si'xpa'tskwin here with this whale he so foolishly led us to. Let him bring it in on his own, or die trying."

The canoe drifted, and the young men became angry that they had been led into such danger. "Let's go home now. Let him stay right on the whale."

They paddled off, these nine young men, and abandoned Si'xpa'tskwin on the carcass. They arrived ashore at the village at Cape Beale late at night when everyone was asleep, but by then they had their story all figured out so that the next day they could explain what had happened.

"Oh, somebody took him," they said. "A canoe came alongside of us, perhaps they were hunting whale. They were people of another tribe, but we don't know which tribe. They took him from our canoe into theirs. There were many in their canoe, and they had many weapons. It was impossible to fight them. So the only thing to do was to flee. It must be that these people had heard of Si'xpa'tskwin's eyes and wanted his sight for themselves."

The people mourned their chief, who had been so mysteriously taken. But Si'xpa'tskwin was not dead. The wind began to blow, first from the east and then from the west. The whale carcass with its stranded passenger drifted even farther out to sea. Si'xpa'tskwin prayed for his life; he prayed that he would go home. He was on the ocean for 10 days, and during this time he heard voices that spoke to him.

"Do not cry, you are slowing us down."

"If you are cold, dig into the blubber and fit yourself down into the hole. Cover your head with the skin, and you will be dry from the rains."

"If your mouth is parched, suck on some blubber. If you are hungry, eat some of the blubber."

In this manner, Si'xpa'tskwin survived. He received good advice from the voices and did not die. All the while he prayed that he be set on land once more. Si'xpa'tskwin knew that spirits were assisting him, but they did not show themselves in true form. At times he thought he saw another canoe with paddlers towing the whale, and once he saw an orca pushing the carcass along. He had many visions and listened to all he was told. Eventually, a voice whispered that the whale was now beached on the rocks beside his village. The voice then told him where to find a ball that he should throw at those who had left him for dead. When the time came, Si'xpa'tskwin threw the ball, which twirled and spun in the air. It landed on the rocks near the carcass and kept spinning. At once it began making a wolf-whistling sound, and at this moment all nine of the young men who had abandoned Si'xpa'tskwin doubled up in pain and died. In this way the spirits helped the chief take revenge on those who had betrayed him.

* * *

Each Huu-ay-aht whaler has his own sacred spots for oosimich, but one of the most sacred spots of all is the mountain known as O'quatsqa, which translates as "Bladder-head." Named for the profile it presents from certain angles, this mountain resembles the inflated seal skins that are used as floats when whaling. The whole mountain is sacred, from the valleys surrounding it to the slopes leading up to its peak and the cliffs that run down to the ocean. The red cedar that grows on this mountain has special qualities not found in cedar from other territories. The mountain is also special because it has many hidden spots that are perfect for performing oosimich. For this reason, it is a destination point. But Bladder-head has another level of importance. On and around this mountain, an unusual group of supernatural spirits resides.

Their power can be dangerous, so travel on the mountain is not for the uninitiated.

The caves of Bladder-head house something quite marvellous and rare. These are He'na', supernatural quartz crystals that grow to a huge size. Very responsive to movement, the He'na' often sway back and forth and at times vibrate, emitting an unusual humming sound. The louder the humming, the greater the power. The ball that Si'xpa'tskwin threw at his betrayers hummed and emitted a whistling sound because it was a crystal, given to him by the spirits who helped him bring the drift whale to shore.

The valleys approaching the mountain are where the Y'ai' can sometimes reveal themselves. But only an observant and quickly responsive person will see them. Farther up the mountain slopes, the Y'ai' hide. These Y'ai' are supernatural spirits who resemble men but have tufts of feathers projecting up from either side of their heads. They are usually seen in groups, in the magical number combinations of 4 or 10, and they emit a shrill sound like children make at play. It is important to be strong spiritually, for the Y'ai' have been known to kill without mercy those who encounter them without proper preparation. Y'ai' dispense power and can infuse one who is ready with special skills in whaling or doctoring, in the arts, or in song. They can even bestow wealth.

It seems as though the Y'ai' are seen more often than two other creatures that reside on the mountain. The

Michtach are odd-shaped, mallard-like birds with beautiful feathers and supernatural powers that people can obtain by snatching part of their plumage. They are among the most unusual supernatural creatures, and accounts of seeing a Michtach, let alone successfully catching a feather, are exceedingly rare. They fly with lightning speed and can swoop down unexpectedly, but it is their noise that is most reported. There are so many of them hidden away that when they flap their wings they make a thunderous sound that can be overwhelming and deafening. A whaler might visit the mountain many times in his life and hear the Michtach, but never get close enough to see them.

Another supernatural creature also resides on the bluffs of Bladder-head Mountain. This is the Ch'och'oht'a, which translates as "stretched down from a bluff onto the rocks." According to the elders, this creature "is said to look like a big octopus, and can give good power for whale-hunting. It is extremely difficult to get. When you get near, he goes right up the bluff out of reach so you cannot get a piece of him for a charm . . . he always stays on rocks. He is black, like a whale, and has many eyes like an octopus."

The following story, told by William to Edward Sapir in 1914, is an important narrative because it is one of only a few sources of traditional information about the sacred mountain that lies within Huu-ay-aht territory. The story shows us the importance of the mountain's supernatural power and spirit creatures in the quest for whaling prowess.

The Happynook family held their last whale hunt in 1928 at Cha'pis. Distributing portions of the butchered whale are, from left to right: Jackson Jack (with his back to the camera), William Dennis, Kenneth Joe (?), Gus Tuutiismis (?) and Gordon Frank. To the right are Billy Happynook and Mexis, with the little boy, and Jack Peter on the far right. HUU-AY-AHT FIRST NATION

An Unlikely Whaler

The village of Yashitko'a lies far inland from the mouth of Barkley Sound, near Coleman Creek. The people of this village were expert canoe makers. They were a very rich people because the work they did was in demand from others and they could trade canoes for almost everything they needed. But in this village was a young chief who did not like it that their neighbours made fun of them. Whaling was a prestigious pursuit, while making canoes from red cedar trees was not, even though it required great skill. The Yashitko'a traded for sea mammals and therefore had no need to oosimich. This made them humble when among those who did. When the Yashitko'a people visited their neighbours, they took gifts of cedar boards for making houses. These boards, made of the finest and straightest-grain cedar, were very well formed but rather pedestrian.

"Don't bother to look in their canoes," the neighbours would say when the Yashitko'a came visiting. "They have only brought us boards for gifts."

The young Yashitko'a chief said to his father, "I want to become a whaler. I want to catch many whales so our village can be proud whalers, not just proud canoe makers."

"Well," his father answered, "to learn to be a whaler, you must make preparation. You must pray and prepare your body and mind. You must bathe in the sacred places; you must fast and stay vigilant, training your mind. This will be a commitment, my son. Are you ready for such a step?"

The young man was ready, and he started oosimich, bathing and rubbing his body with special plants so that he would become strong. He did this every day for a year. At the end of the year he sat beside the small fire that he had built to warm himself. He covered his shoulders with a bearskin robe and stared into the fire. All at once he saw a creature creep to the fire and steal the flames away. The young chief followed this creature and tried to catch it and reclaim the fire. But it seemed that whatever he did, he could not quite catch up to whatever it was that ran ahead of him. As much as he tried, the creature was too quick, and he could only follow at some distance behind it. The creature led him to the mountain called Bladder-head. When he got there, the young man became dizzy and slumped down on the forest floor, passed out. But something brought him back to consciousness and made him wake up.

As he opened his eyes he saw a strange creature, not the creature that had stolen his fire, but another. This one was black and had many hands. In a flash it jumped up the bluff and was gone.

"This is too strange," thought the young man. "Whatever it is has left me here and I am unable to follow." He returned home.

Again, he began oosimich, and again he bathed and prayed, strengthening his body and mind. He had visions. In the visions he saw another creature; this one looked a bit like a cormorant, but made a noise like an otter and also like a mallard duck. The young man told his father about these visions.

"Well my son, you must now continue oosimich for another four days. After this you must walk and travel to the mountain called Bladder-head. You must seek out this creature you have seen, for it is a Michtach. This is a very special being, and one that can provide you with powers also. Each one has powers for different purposes. You must find the Michtach for whalers."

Again the young man walked and reached the valley beside the mountain. He saw all sorts of strange birds flying about. "Surely they are supernatural," he thought to himself. "They sound and look so unusual." He watched carefully, hoping to be able to get close to one of them. But they were very aware of him and did not reveal themselves fully. It was very frustrating for the young chief, and in the end his patience ran out. He became disheartened and returned home, where some of the villagers chided him because he kept coming back with no power. It was embarrassing to listen to their laughter and teasing, but he remained committed and resolved to try again.

Once more the young man performed oosimich, and once more he spoke with his father, who encouraged him in this pursuit. This time, the young man asked that his mother pack four strips of dried blubber that he could take with him for nourishment. He then went upstream along the river and walked all day until dark. He stopped several times to bathe and to tear four small strips off the blubber, which he ate. It took a long while to get to the mountain. He wanted to make sure his body was pure and that his mind was protected from harm. By eating and sucking on the blubber, he was protected by the spirit of the whale, and so he felt strong. Then, as he approached the bluffs, he encountered the Ch'och'oht'a, and again it sped away from him up the mountain. Discouraged, the young man returned home yet another time.

Once more he prepared. But this time he asked his

mother for advice. She looked at her son and saw how strong he was. His body was toughened, his eyes bright, and his heart good. "Maybe," she began, "maybe it is your breath that the beings smell. It gives you away. These beings can smell you and have warning that you are near to them. You offend them with your smell, and they know that you are not worthy. You must disguise the smell of your breath. To do this, my son, you must fast for ten days. Drink only water and then set out once more."

Ten days of fasting focused the young man. He was now very determined, and his mind was made up. This was his fourth trip, and he would not return until he had accomplished the task. This time, he strode out purposefully. When he reached the base of the bluff, he stopped and stood very quietly. After a long while, he saw movement off to the side, and still he waited. The Ch'och'oht'a crept along the rocks and did not appear to notice him. Slowly, ever so slowly, he crouched down, preparing to spring towards the creature. Still the creature made no indication that it had seen him.

"I must be worthy," he reminded himself. "I must not offend the Ch'och'oht'a with my smell, or my breath."

He judged the timing and in one quick movement grabbed for the creature. This time he caught the tip of one of its arms. He held tight as the creature wiggled and squirmed. With mighty strength, the creature pulled away, but left behind in the young man's hands some pieces of its tentacle.

"Success!" he cried aloud. "Thank you, Great Spirit, for preparing me to be worthy." And with that thought, the young man carefully wrapped his power in a soft skin and turned back for the homeward journey. Just outside the village, close to his house, the young man found a secret spot in which to hide his power, for it was forbidden to take the charm into a house. He then entered the house and all his family gathered around him. They could tell from his demeanour that he was changed and now had supernatural power.

Four days passed. On the fourth day, the young man advised, "Today the humpbacks will come into the bay."

The young man went with others from the village down to the beach and into the canoes. That day, he caught four whales, killing each one with only a single spear thrust. The young man was now a proven whaler. He had achieved his aspiration, and now his village could be proud. Not only were the Yashitko'a people famous as canoe makers, but their young chief also had great powers as a whaler. They would never be hungry because he could charm the whales right into the bay.

7

The World Changes Forever

WHEN THE BRITISH MAN-OF-WAR HMS *Constance* dropped anchor in Esquimalt Harbour near the colonial capital of Victoria on Vancouver Island in 1848, a new and irresistible military presence became a reality of life for the Huu-ay-aht and all other Native people in the region. William Eddie Banfield, one of *Constance*'s crew, cast his eyes ashore and judged the wild and free-for-all ambience of the small colonial settlement of Victoria to be exactly to his liking. When he discharged from the British naval service at Victoria in 1849, he eagerly turned his hand to a new career in trading. Together with partner Peter Francis, Banfield purchased a small sloop named *Leonede*. During the 1850s, Banfield and Francis plied the waters of the west coast of Vancouver

Island from Port San Juan to Quatsino Sound, purchasing furs, pelts and dogfish oil from the Native tribes in exchange for blankets, tools, beads and other manufactured goods.

Banfield learned to speak Nuu-chah-nulth and became familiar with all the tribes of the coast, including the Huu-ay-aht and their chief, Tliishin. Banfield and Francis became the local white experts on West Coast life, penning a number of informative letters to Governor Douglas and reports for the Victoria newspapers. In 1855, they reported to Douglas that the Huu-ay-aht numbered about 500 people in all, including about 180 able-bodied men, and that they were "not disposed seemingly to treat Whites with much kindness, it may be accounted for by not having much intercourse with them." Little did Banfield suspect that intercourse with the Huu-ay-aht would soon become the central element of his life.

The captain and crew of the rickety brig *Swiss Boy* knew that February 1, 1859, would be a bad day. Overloaded with timber, *Swiss Boy* wallowed under sail into Barkley Sound with the planking of her hull coming apart, taking on water and in danger of sinking. The vessel maneuvered its way onto a mid-channel rock in an effort to prevent the complete loss of her cargo and crew. Several canoes of Huu-ay-aht people followed the course of the stricken vessel, carefully watching to see where it would land. Once *Swiss Boy* settled on the rocks, the Huu-ay-aht pounced, claiming the vessel, her crew and all goods aboard to be their property as honi, or drift goods. Within Native traditional law, any whales or other drift goods that floated to shore became the property of the chief and tribe who owned the hahoothlee—thus *Swiss Boy* fit the bill.

Chief Tliishin and another Huu-ay-aht named George took command of the proceedings, directing canoes to tow the stricken vessel onto another reef in front of two Huu-ay-aht villages. The Huu-ay-aht soon stripped the vessel of any items they valued and held the crew for ransom as customary tradition dictated. When news of the plight of *Swiss Boy* and her crew reached Governor Douglas in Victoria, he dispatched the British gunboat *Satellite* to investigate. When he had Huu-ay-aht villages and people under direct threat from *Satellite*'s cannons, Captain Prevost was able to negotiate with Chief Tliishin for the safe release of *Swiss Boy*'s crew and recovered much of her cargo as well; all in exchange for 40 trade blankets. Captain Prevost recognized that the Huu-ay-aht had acted as they did because of their customary law, but he also made it clear to Tliishin and the Huu-ay-aht that, in future, British law was also to be respected. Later, Prevost reported to Governor Douglas, making a strong recommendation that an "Indian Agent" should be appointed for Barkley Sound, to prevent any future misunderstandings.

With plans afoot for investors to build and operate a forestry mill in Barkley Sound, along with schemes for colonization in the area, Douglas decided to act on Prevost's recommendation. Douglas selected trader Banfield as the ideal candidate for Indian Agent for the southwest coast of Vancouver Island. Banfield swore an oath of allegiance on April 28, 1859, and, as a requirement of his duties, sought to establish a residence in Barkley Sound. Banfield soon determined that Huu-ay-aht territory would be the best place to live, but he was also aware that he must negotiate arrangements with Chief Tliishin to settle in the chief's hahoothlee. On July 6, 1859, the Huu-ay-aht established their first agreement for lands with an outsider: "Ohiaht Barclay Sound . . . I William Eddy Banfield Government Agent for the Western Shore of Vancouver Island have this day . . . bought of Cleeshin the Chief of Ohiaht and Howeesem the next in rank of the same tribe that Island known among the tribe by the name of Osometticey, all and every part of it for the sum and consideration of two blankets and two shirts its water privileges and timber to be mine forever my heirs and assigns [*sic*] for the aforesaid sum of two blankets and two shirts which these chiefs have acknowledged by affixing the marks and seals here under on which this is the title deed each of aforesaid chiefs holding a copy. [signed] Cleeshins mark and seal Howeesems mark and seal Witness Howeesems son." Chiefs Tliishin and Howeesem confirmed their assent by affixing strips of sacred cedar bark to this agreement with sealing wax.

It seems doubtful that Banfield had fully explained the terms of this agreement to Tliishin, since according to Huu-ay-aht laws only a chief could hold the rights to land,

This 1859 agreement for land use was signed by Chief Tliishin using an X made of sacred cedar.

though these rights could be temporarily assigned to fellow tribesmen; Tliishin likely considered Banfield's payments as rent or homage rather than purchase.

Banfield established his trading post in what is now Bamfield Inlet, but as some animosity developed between Banfield and the Huu-ay-aht chiefs, he later moved his base of operations to nearby Grappler Inlet. In October 1862, after Banfield's drowned body was found floating near his residence off Grappler Inlet, accusations of foul play were raised in the Victoria press, with suspicions cast particularly on Chief Tliishin. For months afterward, white traders spread rumours that gunboats would come to avenge Banfield's death by bombarding Huu-ay-aht villages and killing all the Huu-ay-aht they could find. The tribe lived in great fear, as the terrible news of gunboat attacks on other Native villages along the coast had spread far and wide.

Eventually, a gunboat was indeed dispatched in September 1864 to secure those accused in Banfield's death. When advance warning reached the Huu-ay-aht, they expected the worst; together they determined to make a last stand to protect their chief, their village and their people. The British navy gunboat *Devastation* steamed up Barkley Sound, anchored off the Huu-ay-aht village of Numukamis, ran out their cannons and trained them ashore. A boat was lowered from *Devastation*, loaded with armed policemen prepared to arrest those accused of Banfield's murder. As the police boat approached the village, many canoes of Huu-ay-aht warriors, dressed and armed for battle, appeared from hiding behind a headland and quickly surrounded the police boat, threatening violence to those aboard. The Huu-ay-aht seized one of the policemen as a hostage for security, then sent a delegation to board *Devastation* and negotiate terms. Once it was agreed that only those accused of murder would be sought, that their village would not be bombarded and that a fair trial would occur, the Huu-ay-aht ceased hostilities and released their hostage.

Three Huu-ay-aht men accused of the murder were taken in custody aboard *Devastation* for transport to Victoria, along with Tliishin's daughter as a hostage to induce the chief himself to surrender to the colonial authorities. When the case was called before the Chief Justice in Victoria in November 1864, Klatsmick alone stood accused of Banfield's murder, and Tliishin was there to provide testimony. Despite witnesses who stated that Klatsmick had told them he had stabbed Banfield, the Chief Justice found the evidence to be weak; Klatsmick was acquitted.

The *Swiss Boy* affair and the Banfield murder case made it clear to the Huu-ay-aht that their world had changed forever. The British colonial power could and would use its military superiority and firepower to achieve its ends.

In 1871, British Columbia joined Confederation, and the federal government of Canada assumed jurisdiction over Indian Affairs. In 1874, George Blenkinsop was hired by the Superintendent of Indian Affairs and travelled to Barkley Sound on the west coast of Vancouver Island. His job was "to gather information on Native needs and desires with regard to land" as a preparation for the allocation of "Indian Reservations," which would be undertaken by a duly-appointed Indian Reserve Commission. Blenkinsop spent three months travelling by boat and on foot. During this time, he interviewed the chiefs of each tribe to learn about their use of the land for food gathering, their traditions in hunting both on the ocean and in the forest, and all manner of resource extraction. He recorded the names of each family in each lodge, as well as the ages and sex of all family members. This was the first formal census of Barkley Sound, for these First Nations had no such need to record their family information on paper. They had traditional historians who kept track.

But the government needed the paper records. The purpose, of course, was to see how many people lived in the area and on what land they resided. With this information in hand, government officials could then send the Reserve Commissioner and surveyors to measure out the land reservations for the First Nations. This land would be held in trust for them, while other adjacent lands could be purchased or pre-empted by the outsiders: the white immigrants, the merchants, the entrepreneurs and the timber barons.

Blenkinsop was a patient and experienced man. He wanted to make sure he understood how Huu-ay-aht society

In September 1874, Dr. I.W. Powell, Superintendent of Indian Affairs, travelled to Barkley Sound and met with delegations of Huu-ay-aht people. It is thought that this photograph, taken on board HMS *Boxer*, portrays the Huu-ay-aht party led by their chief, Adzik, Chief Louie's grandfather. George Blenkinsop, who had taken the census of Huu-ay-aht people that spring, is shown on the far right.

worked and how the land and its resources were used. He asked many questions and spoke to chiefs from different villages. He could see that the large territory in which the Huu-ay-aht lived was not all filled with people. In fact, he wrote to Ottawa to say that based upon his observations of the size and quantity of abandoned villages, "incontestably the population of Barkley Sound must have been at no very remote period, ten times its present number." He also noted that people lived in villages on a seasonal basis, following the food cycle and the weather. Thus, he wrote, "It is difficult to obtain an accurate accounting of the population because many of the people are between villages, or have just moved from one site to the next, and I have missed them." When Blenkinsop recorded his census, many of the large villages on the salmon-bearing rivers were not inhabited, because, of course, it was summer and most salmon had not yet returned to the rivers to spawn.

The census results proved what First Nations had known for some time: their once robust population was but a shadow of its former self. Yes, natural cataclysms such as earthquakes, flooding and violent storms had taken lives. And yes, the human dynamic and the friction of the many tribes within Barkley Sound were taken into account, as groups jostled for rights to hunting areas, salmon streams and drift whales. But what Blenkinsop was observed was not a minor or general weakening of the population base. He was seeing the remnants of what had been populous tribes,

tribes whose decreased numbers echoed the experiences of other Nuu-chah-nulth peoples in Clayoquot and Nootka Sounds, and indeed along the Pacific coast generally.

Today, historians estimate that by the mid-19th century, the population of First Nations on the coast of British Columbia had been decimated by at least 90 percent. This massive depopulation occurred within a single generation and was a direct result of contact with the outsider society—the explorers and early maritime fur traders—who brought infectious diseases such as measles, whooping cough, tuberculosis, influenza, syphilis, and the most deadly of all, smallpox. First Nations people had no immunity to these diseases, which were unknown in their world.

In the few years between Cook's 1778 sojourn at Nootka Sound and Simon Fraser's overland journey to the coast in 1808, it was obvious that the area's First Peoples had been stricken by epidemics that had travelled the length of the coast. The sicknesses had passed from the outsiders to First Nations, but then spread through trade and contact between the First Nations themselves. The first European reference to introduced disease dates from 1791, when the log from the ship *Columbia* records that smallpox was present among the Nuu-chah-nulth: "Twas evident that these Natives had been visited by that scourge of mankind. The Smallpox ... The face of the Chief bears evident marks."

In 1788, fur-trader John Meares calculated the number of people under the authority of the major Nuu-chah-nulth chiefs in Barkley, Clayoquot and Nootka Sounds. The total number came to 31,000. Even roughly dividing by three, this estimates a robust population within Barkley Sound itself. But in 1874, less than 100 years later, Blenkinsop was only able to confirm that 949 people lived in all of Barkley Sound. And of these, the once mighty Huu-ay-aht now numbered only 262.

A Huu-ay-aht account records a specific instance when smallpox came to their territory. It was at the end of the Long War, and the tribes in Barkley Sound had agreed to stop fighting. But suspicions and uncertainty still coloured people's perceptions regarding the motives of others.

Smallpox

The story begins when a ship came to N'aqowis, across from Bamfield Inlet. The ship did not anchor, but seemed instead to drift about as though no one was onboard. This was quite curious and out of character for these mamatni, or outsiders, who were usually so regulated and assertive. However, from the Huu-ay-aht perspective, custom demanded that they greet each visitor to their territory. As usual, they organized a procession of canoes that went out to the ship.

"Welcome!" they called as their canoes came close to the hull. But there was no answering call. Unworried, the villagers climbed aboard. When they stood on the deck and looked down the hatch, they saw that there was something very wrong with many of the white sailors, for they were all groaning. The ship had come up the coast from San Francisco, and the captain told them that it had already stopped in at Yuquot and at Ahousat.

The captain turned to the Huu-ay-aht and said, "For seven days you will be well. Then you will get that sickness." The Huu-ay-aht did not know what the sickness was, as they had not seen it before. Within the seven days, they knew all about it, for this was smallpox. Many died. Out of 2,000 adults, only 80 families survived.

The Huu-ay-aht grew suspicious. Why, if the crew had been so sick, had the ship ventured into villages on the coast? Had they been seeking assistance, or had something more nefarious been planned? Some of the Huu-ay-aht thought it had been a deliberate exposure and believed their enemies, the Clallam people, had directed the American sailors to come north.

Many Huu-ay-aht died over the next six months. Chief Louie's grandfather, who had not been on the ship, quickly moved his family to a mountain near Sarita Lake. By doing so, they escaped the smallpox. Eventually, the sickness ended. There was much talk among the survivors, for all were convinced that the American captain had been hired to spread the disease. The Huu-ay-aht talked with the Ucluelet, who, until the close of the Long War, had been their bitter enemies. The Ucluelet, too, had suffered and were angry. Together, the two groups formed a war party and went to Clallam Bay to take revenge. Just how they did this, however, is unclear. It is not recorded whether the attack was successful, but with such a reduction in population, none of the survivors had the resources or abilities to mount and carry out an effective raid.

* * *

In 1868, missionary Harry Guillod reported on an outbreak of smallpox among the Huu-ay-aht: "40 Huu-ay-ahts had died of the disease which was fast spreading . . . those who were affected by it were so terrified that they were neglecting to lay in their winter's store of salmon, so that starvation would probably ensue upon the disease." In 1881, Guillod, now the Indian Agent, conducted his first actual census. He travelled throughout Barkley, Clayoquot and Nootka Sounds and counted 3,610 people, confirming a 90 percent reduction in population.

It is difficult to imagine the personal psychological impact, let alone the cultural impact, of losing 9 out of every 10 people within a 50-year period. Who would raise the children? Who would bury the dead? Who would own the rights and prerogatives if a family was wiped out? How would the oral history of the people survive? How would the intricate sharing of resources and communal gathering of foods continue? Who would teach the young men how to prepare themselves for catching whales? Who would build the canoes and dry the salmon?

Many proud and numerous lineages were swept away.

The traditional independence of the local groups could not continue without enough people. Instead, the survivors forged alliances with neighbouring villages, sharing village sites and territories. The world of the Huu-ay-aht was forever changed.

The remaining peoples still held the rights to the traditional territories and privileges. They were hard-pressed to make Blenkinsop understand that their system of land use and occupation required the large geographical areas of the territories they claimed. In Blenkinsop's view, the future for First Nations lay not in maintaining their old way of life, but in embracing the new order controlled by the outsider society and its government. The Huu-ay-aht and other nations were expected to develop agriculture, to grow potatoes, to plant fruit trees and to tend the land at a specific spot. Blenkinsop and others of the day believed that the old ways would die out and that assimilation with the outsider society was not only desired but inevitable.

Blenkinsop drew a map of Barkley Sound and marked on it the areas in which he found people situated. He did listen and take into consideration the information they provided about the places that salmon and other foods were harvested. He recommended that the government surveyors measure out modest plots of land on whatever arable areas people happened to already live on and also allow for small encampment areas on salmon rivers and for burials—lots of burials. The sizes of these reserves were small and often included infertile or inhospitable areas.

Peter O'Reilly was the Indian Reserve Commissioner who was sent the following year to meet with representatives of the Huu-ay-aht. He steamed up from Victoria on a naval ship and arrived in Dodger's Cove on Diana Island on May 26, 1882. The next day, he recorded the following in his diary: "Had an interview with the chiefs of the Huu-ay-aht tribe. Afterwards accompanied by them I laid off a number of reserves nearly all for fishing purposes. Intended to go to Bamfield Cr. but could not, returned to Dodger's Cove." The following day was Sunday, and he remained on board the ship writing letters home and observing the "day of rest." On Monday: "Up anchor at 5:45 a.m. A lovely morning. Laid out a reserve at Helby Island and then steamed to Bamfield Creek . . . Worked hard all the day and anchored in Green Cove at 7:30 p.m." He was now out of Huu-ay-aht territory, and on to the next tribe's reservations. He spent a total of two days actually speaking with and visiting the Huu-ay-aht and their villages. On the basis of this short interaction and with little actual time spent in the vicinity, O'Reilly laid out 13 small land reserves for the Huu-ay-aht.

The people were now forced onto these small plots of land, spread throughout their territory, and denied access to or use of most of their traditional sites. It is estimated that these Huu-ay-aht Indian Reserves represented less than 1 percent of the territory they once controlled. These reserves were never given to the Huu-ay-aht, but held in trust for them by the government of Canada. Such a paternalistic view was intolerable for the Huu-ay-aht, but what could a formerly strong people do? The laws of British Columbia denied them the right to own land, yet outsiders could pre-empt and purchase any of the Huu-ay-aht lands not included in these 13 reserves. It was intolerable.

On May 8, 1914, Chief Louie and other Huu-ay-aht elders spoke to the members of the Joint Federal-Provincial Indian Commission when it came to Bamfield to meet with the Huu-ay-aht. This was part of a longer trip in which the commissioners travelled around British Columbia to speak with all First Nations about the reservations that had been established between 1874 and 1912.

In the few scant hours they were there, the commissioners asked Chief Louie and other Huu-ay-aht chiefs questions about their land allotments. In the outsider community, there was some speculation that these reserves were too large for the needs of First Nations and should be cut back. Chief Louie was not impressed with the interchange. The commissioners posed very specific questions concerning the use of the land, but asked about agricultural use, not evidence of use that was traditional to the Huu-ay-aht. They asked about seasonal villages, about gas boats, about sealing (which by then was outlawed) and about schooling. They did not seem to require in-depth responses and, in fact, did not encourage detail. Finally, near the end of the interviews, Chief Louie made a point of illustrating the differences between Huu-ay-aht traditional fishing and the fishing practised by the Japanese and white people who had moved in and pre-empted or purchased land that was on the more significant Huu-ay-aht sites. These people freely moved—without permission of the Huu-ay-aht, but with the protection of the outsider society—in the waters which had for generations been the prerogatives of chiefs.

"The cannery men are using a seine for their fishing," Chief Louie explained, "and they catch all the fish going up the Sarita River. They purchase a licence for the seine and they place the nets in such a manner that we in our gas boats trolling or, on our land at Numukamis, are unable to fish, for all the salmon are caught in the nets before they can swim up the river. This is a serious situation, for our people cannot catch the salmon we need because the seine nets catch the salmon. I worry for my people, and I worry for the survival of the salmon. Never before have such quantities of salmon been caught before they spawn. Tell me, will you do something about this?"

One commissioner replied, "This question of closing the mouths of streams by seines was discussed by the commission with the federal and provincial government fishery officers a short time ago."

The other commissioner then added: "We will take everything you have told us today into consideration and will do what we can for you."

With that final remark, the representatives closed their books and adjourned the meeting. Chief Louie never received an answer. Fifty years later, his anger at that day remained unabated. Sitting in front of a microphone and tape recorder, he paused in his storytelling to remind his listeners of these historical injustices. He spoke of his father's attempts to stop the surveyors and of the hollow promises given by the commissioner and government officials. "Now the government surveyors are taking our lands. They are putting us on tiny reservations, all these lands we owned. The lands surrounding us are literally taken away from us. Dr. Powell was head of the Indian Commission in 1874–76. My father went to the surveyor in 1875–76. He confronted him, asking, 'How can you give us small piece of land in our own territory? What are you surveyors doing by taking and stealing our lands?'

"My father was very concerned but did not want to fight the government. He only asked 'How can they take our lands?' The government said we wouldn't lose our lands, and we would still have all the rights. 'You'll never be in need of wood. You'll still be able to use all your resources, such as cedar for making canoes. When you have to go into the forest you can still make your canoes. Whatever it takes to build. You can fall all the cedar you want for canoes or firewood, because this is your territory. If you want to build your long houses, or cut shingles the cedar is there for you to harvest.' This is what Dr. Powell said in Victoria. The government will give you cattle, sheep, pigs—even give us chickens and let them multiply and make money on this livestock. Dr. Powell said this is good offering for us. [He] said we could have an easier way of living. Yet this never arrived, promise broken again, nothing came from Victoria. This is what the government now claims, that they have claimed our territories without even signing any papers or agreement. No documents. They were just telling us lies so they could benefit for themselves. All the chiefs witnessed this, fooling us in what they promised.

"The surveyors still went ahead and placed us on small reserves and stole our lands. All the money came from Ottawa, thousands and thousands of dollars, but we did not get any of it. We did not sell our lands. Because our lands are too valuable to our people. Yet the government never treated us right. They took our lands. Our chiefs never signed them away."

These Indian Reserves became the only lands allocated to the Huu-ay-aht for over 125 years and were just a few tiny parcels making up a very small percentage of their territory. In 2009, the Huu-ay-aht, as part of the Maa-nulth First Nations, reached a final agreement with British Columbia and Canada, and regained control over a much more substantial portion of their lands.

CHAPTER

8

Fur Sealing

THE ADULT MALE NORTHERN FUR SEAL is huge, weighing 270 kilograms and measuring 2.5 metres long. In contrast, the female is tiny, weighing 45 kilograms and measuring 1.3 metres long. These remarkable animals live most of their lives in the ocean, coming onto land only to mate and give birth. They are resident from California to Alaska, and each spring a large population once swam north, migrating to the Pribilof Islands, where they bred. However, not all fur seals migrated; some stayed all year in Huu-ay-aht territory. This was once an important benefit for the Huu-ay-aht, as it was much easier to hunt close to home.

Fur seals have a rich, warm pelt. Given the damp, cold winters on the coast, these pelts were ideal for clothing. The large male animals also provided food for the people. In the Huu-ay-aht world view, it is crucial to keep the balance in nature, to ensure that human needs do not jeopardize or overpower those of nature. All is one. It is important to honour the life of the animal you kill for food. The way you respect the animal is to ensure there is no waste, that all of the animal is utilized once it is killed, and that it did not give its life needlessly.

Not every Huu-ay-aht man had the right to hunt seals. The right was given and handed down within families, as was the right to fish for salmon on particular spots on the river, as was the right to hunt whales. Those who held the rights also held the responsibility to be providers for others and to share.

The Huu-ay-aht hunted seals using spears that measured four or five metres long and about three centimetres in diameter. The spears had a handle and two fastened-on prongs, one almost a metre long and the other half this length. The shafts were made of crabapple wood and the spear points of mussel shells, deer and elk horn, or stone. As trade goods came into the territory from the outsiders, metal commonly replaced these natural materials as the preferred spearhead.

Because the seals lived in the ocean, they were generally speared from canoes. These dugout cedar canoes were specially designed with flat bottoms for stability, flared gunwales on the bow to prevent water from splashing, and high vertical sterns. After contact, the Huu-ay-aht experimented by adding sails of canvas or cotton. This allowed the paddlers to rest when the wind was strong and enabled the canoes to travel farther offshore. The seals resident in Huu-ay-aht territory were also sometimes speared from shore as they basked on the rocks at low tide.

The first mamatni, or outsiders, saw a commercial use for the pelts of the fur seals, the sea otter and fur-bearing land mammals. In many world centres, especially those in China and Europe, these furs became valued commodities. Thus, a brisk maritime trade commenced between merchants who arrived on ships and the coastal First Nations who exchanged fur pelts for beads, metal, cloth and food-stuffs. As more ships arrived on the coast, the pressure to provide fur pelts for trade created a dilemma for the Huu-ay-aht and others. How could they maintain their world view when an extraordinary demand for furs from these outsiders pressured the community into compromising the balance of resource consumption?

No longer was their economy self-sufficient, based on trading within First Nations and living off the bounty of nature. Now, new goods and foods entered the picture and outside influences (like the infectious diseases that killed so many) initiated change that came so rapidly the Huu-ay-aht were swept up in it before they realized it could not be controlled.

As the quest for furs became big business, consortiums

based in San Francisco and Victoria financed a fleet of sailing vessels that followed the seals north and killed them when they were most vulnerable—on land at the rookeries where they bred and gave birth. Huu-ay-aht people were in demand as sealers. The sailing vessels took their canoes and crew on board with them as they sailed north. The sealers were paid for each seal speared, but not paid in cash, just in foodstuffs and trading goods. For several intense decades in the late 19th century, sealing provided a living for many Huu-ay-aht men. Young men grew up learning not the old ways, but the new ways of sealing—of hunting for goods instead of hunting for food. Not surprisingly, despite international attempts to regulate the carnage and killing at the rookeries, the once plentiful fur seals were soon in danger of extinction.

International interests from beyond the Huu-ay-aht world—of business, of investors and of governments—came into play. By 1911, the big business of fur sealing was put under strict regulation and controlled by American and Russian interests. Quotas and international law prevailed. The early settlers had valued the hunting skills of the Huu-ay-aht, as it was tricky business spearing seals from canoes, and the Huu-ay-aht had perfected this work through generations of training. But these skills were no longer needed when guns became the preferred killing tool.

What had once been a pelagic, or ocean-based, hunt became strictly land based and regulated. Native sealers were left out, forbidden to go north on the boats. The people who had become dependent upon this outside employment now had no work. They had no means to purchase goods, and had grown away from the traditional ways of living self-sufficiently within their territory. A time of great hardship followed.

Written histories of sealing generally revolve around the non-Aboriginal participants and focus on the businesses, the sealing captains, the consortiums, the international players and the big-money investments. Chief Louie, however, gives an account from the Huu-ay-aht perspective and discusses his own personal odyssey.

The End of the Seal Hunt

"I was born in 1881 on the 15th of March at Dodger's Cove Island; that's where I was born. In 1894, I had my first experience in going out to the ocean in a sealing canoe to learn how to hunt for fur seals in our territory.

"When we hunted the fur seals we saved the pelts and meat, which was smoked and eaten fresh. This was our tradition to go for these fur seals, this all belongs to us, the people along the coast. We also used [the seals'] hides for our clothing. We did not have to go too far out in the sea because it was so plentiful. The fur seal and hair seal were sometimes some distance out in the ocean, but these seals had mated and bred right here in Huu-ay-aht territory. They didn't migrate north to have their young, although many others did—all along the coast right up to the Bering Sea. We had many seals that stayed in our territory and bred in our waters.

"When I started hunting fur seals I accompanied my father and my older brother. I witnessed the way they speared these seals and soon, the way they hunted these seals. We only took what we needed, that is our way.

"But now two men came, traders, they came in schooners from Victoria. These traders came into our territory and offered the people rice and sugar and molasses in exchange for seals. Their prices for the seals were almost insulting. They used small teacups to measure. A small seal went for two cups of rice. One big fur seal went for three cups of molasses. A white whiskered seal, two cups of molasses or whatever you wanted to purchase in equal value of rice or sugar. These traders came for all the furs—for fur seals, beavers and sea otter. Beaver went for half a cup of rice. Then they brought pants, cotton pants made in China, and the price rose—one seal for one pair of pants.

"Fur seal became big business. We hunted in our own territories. For me and my father, it was the Dodger's Cove area. Now the people hunted seals for trade, we became dependent upon the traders, and the pay for each seal was so small, we killed more than we ever had before. Soon people along the coast had lots of rice, sugar, molasses and pants. But the seals were scarce.

"The white traders were the ones to benefit by all the fur seals. They got wealthy. As long as the seal market was on, we never got a fair shake, because the traders then sold the seals for high prices in Victoria. White people wanted the fur—and the oil—and paid the traders with money. The traders never paid us money, just rice and sugar and such.

"A few years later, though, Captain Victor Jacobson arrived. The name of his schooner was *Kwachisht.* He asked the people to come with him to hunt in the great ocean. Four of our canoes with a Nuu-chah-nulth crew went in the schooner with him. We went to the Bering Sea to spear seals. Captain Jacobson paid us with money for the seals we speared. The price from Captain Jacobson was $2.50 for a fur seal up to 4 or 5 feet in length. He understood our heritage. He told us that he wanted to buy these seals with money and to be honest with us.

"He stationed his schooner off Dodger's Cove. My father and Captain Jacobson became close; my father started looking after the sales of these seals. Soon I started as a crew member on the schooner, and I went with Captain Jacobson every year to hunt seals in the Bering Sea. We brought our canoes on the deck of the schooner when we sailed north, and then when we reached the breeding grounds we lowered the canoes into the water. Two men in each canoe. Lots of our people went with the schooners from Victoria. They did this for a living. It was very common work because of our talent for canoeing and hunting. So when I was growing up I always went with Jacobson. But in 1910 the schooners quit sealing, then the government closed the seal hunt. We were told that we no longer were allowed to hunt fur seals. To do so would be to break the white man's law. It was a very bad time. We had become so dependent on working for the white hunters that we now had no money to buy food from the traders' stores, and the seals were almost all gone. Some fur seals we could still see in our territory, but we were told that we could not kill them, even to feed our families. We were now poor. We had never been poor before because the fur seal supplied our food and clothing and balance was maintained. We were now frightened to voice our concerns. We received no compensation."

The Heart of the People: A Modern Treaty

RECENTLY, THE HUU-AY-AHT HAVE worked hard to preserve their traditional territories. Over the many decades since the outsiders arrived and changed their world, great harm has come to the environment and to the Huu-ay-aht themselves, who were almost obliterated because of disease and alienation from most of their resources and territory. Their culture and traditional knowledge were nearly lost. Gradually, the Huu-ay-aht have grown in number, and many have left the territory, moving away from the small reserves defined in the late 19th century. But they have recently taken bold steps to control their future. The Huu-ay-aht language is now taught in local schools, and the knowledge of the elders is preserved by the modern means of audio and video recordings and computer files. A new pride in their heritage has changed the way they interact with their neighbours.

One important project symbolizing this rebirth was an ambitious scheme undertaken to halt the ecological destruction of the land. Logging and fishing during the 1940s and 1950s took much from the land and the ocean and did not give anything back. Clear-cut logging allowed the hillsides to erode, took away wildlife and damaged salmon streams. Unregulated commercial fishing reduced the numbers of salmon and other fish stocks. The Huu-ay-aht could no longer live off the land, as had been their traditional way. Losing this intimate connection to the land contributed to the loss of their own cultural knowledge. Each generation became more distantly removed from understanding in their hearts the world view expressed by Chief Louie of Hishuk Tsaawak, "all is one," and Isaak, "respect."

To return their people to greatness, the Huu-ay-aht understand that their land must first be healed. Starting in 2000, they organized partnerships with government and industry to begin the work of restoring the Sarita River as a major salmon-bearing river. This would be a costly project and a lengthy one. But even more than money and time, such projects require great faith and personal commitment from all concerned.

To afford the Sarita restoration, the Huu-ay-aht needed to find financing. The only feasible way to obtain the necessary funds involved an extremely emotional decision, but one that in the larger view seemed entirely appropriate. The Huu-ay-aht determined that they would have to use their sacred wood. By selectively logging some of their great red cedars, those trees so integral to their traditional lives, money was raised to help bring back the river, to reclaim it for all. The Sarita is now being restored, and once again some salmon run up it each autumn to spawn. Soon, the Huu-ay-aht believe, the salmon will once more be abundant. The Sarita is the "heart of the people." It is the largest of the 35 rivers and streams in their traditional territories, and is the first to be healed; others will follow. The Huu-ay-ahts' success in the early stages of healing the Sarita marks a new chapter in their long history. The Huu-ay-aht have begun to show the way for other First Nations and to provide a model for the future.

On December 9, 2006, the Huu-ay-aht First Nation initialled a final agreement with the Province of British Columbia and the Government of Canada that concluded many years of negotiations to hammer out a modern treaty that secures the Huu-ay-aht's exclusive rights to significant areas of land in their traditional territory and recognizes continued economic, governance and cultural roles throughout the hahoothlee of the Huu-ay-aht Ha'wiith. The treaty also includes provisions for self-government and rights to resources that include wildlife, fish, timber and minerals. The Huu-ay-aht negotiated their treaty as part of the Maa-nulth First Nations on Vancouver Island, together

The House of Huu-ay-aht at Anacla, opened in 2000, features modern carvings of the Huu-ay-aht welcome figures. Standing in front of the house are, from left to right: Jack Lohman, Royal BC Museum CEO; Angela Wesley, Royal BC Museum board member and a member of the Huu-ay-aht First Nation; and author Kathryn Bridge. KEVIN NEARY

with the Ka:'yu:'k't'h'/Chek'tles7et'h' First Nations, the Toquaht Nation, the Uchucklesaht Tribe and the Ucluelet First Nation.

On April 1, 2011, the Huu-ay-aht treaty came into full effect. In addition to the small parcels of land that had been allotted as Indian Reserves by Reserve Commissioner O'Reilly in 1881, the Huu-ay-aht regained control over several much larger tracts of land in their territory. Significantly, the largest parcels of land returned to the

Huu-ay-aht are clustered along the Sarita River and its valley, the Heart of the People.

The Huu-ay-aht's treaty is founded on two key traditional concepts, those of Isaak and Hishuk Tsawaak. Larry Johnson, Director of Lands and Natural Resources for the Huu-ay-aht First Nations, explains how these important philosophies, handed down through countless generations, continue to guide all decision making for the Huu-ay-aht. "Isaak is interpreted as 'respect' but it is much more than that—it's a way of life, it's how you carry yourself, it's how you want people to treat you. The words Hishuk Tsawaak mean 'everything is connected.' What you do here will impact over there, so when you combine those two philosophies, you come up with what to me it means to be a Huu-ay-aht, what it means to be connected to our land and to our resources. Managing our lands and natural resources is a vital part of creating a better life for present and future Huu-ay-aht citizens."

The Huu-ay-aht treaty has brought with it many changes that are visible throughout their community at Anacla and beyond. A beautiful new tribal administration building is now perched above the Pachena River, next to the House of Huu-ay-aht, featuring stunning views over the Pachena River valley, Pachena Bay and beyond out to the Pacific Ocean. Numerous plans are in place, including those to develop more housing for Huu-ay-aht citizens in the same area, above the flood plain of the river below and the ever-present threat from tsunamis such as that which carried away the people of Luh'taa over two centuries ago.

The Huu-ay-aht have started on a new journey, their course guided by the lessons of the past and the wisdom, strength and resolve of the ancestors and elders who brought them to this new point of departure. After 140 years of living under an Indian Act imposed by outsiders, the Huu-ay-aht have embarked on a voyage that allows them to regain strength every day, every year and every decade. The vision of the treaty, to regain control of their lands, lives and resources, will unfold throughout the years to come.

Glossary of Place Names

For the ease of most readers, place names and other Native words in the accounts are rendered in an approximate spelling in English of how these words sound in the Huu-ay-aht language. For accuracy, place names are presented here in their Native linguistic transcription. Current "common" place names are provided where such exist.

English	Linguistic	"Common" name
Anacla	ʔaanaqƛa	Anacla
Cha'pis	čapʔis	Dodger's Cove
Ch'ima'tokosoa	čimataqsuʔa	Cape Beale
Clutus	ƚuutas	Clutus
Kaka'apiya	kakaʼpiya	
Keeha	kiixaa	Keeha
Kee'hin	kiixin	Keeshan
Keekee'hinkook	kikiixʔinkʼuk	
Malsit	maƚsit	Malsit
Mugh-yuu	muuqḥyuu	Broughton Peaks
Luh'taa	ƚuhʼtaa	
Nanaskiyis	nanaskiyis	Brady's Beach
N'aqowis	naquwis	
Numukamis	nuumaqimyis	Numukamis, Sarita
O'quatsqa	ʔoːʔquatsqa	
Ots'o'a	ʔucuʔua	
Tl'itsnit	ƛʼitsnit	
Wihata	wiḥaataʔa	
Yashitko'a	yašitquua	Coleman Creek

Bibliography

Arima, Eugene. *The West Coast (Nootka) People.* Victoria: British Columbia Provincial Museum, 1983.

Arima, Eugene, and Denis St. Claire. *Between Ports Alberni and Renfrew: Notes on West Coast Peoples.* Hull, PQ: Canadian Museum of Civilization, 1991.

Arima, Eugene, Henry Kammler, Terry Klokeid, and Katherine Robinson, eds. *Family Origin Histories: The Whaling Indians, West Coast Legends and Stories.* Hull, PQ: Canadian Museum of Civilization, 2009.

Arima, Eugene, Terry Klokeid, and Katherine Robinson, eds. *The Whaling Indians, West Coast Legends and Stories: Tales of Extraordinary Experience.* Hull, PQ: Canadian Museum of Civilization, 2000.

Harris, R. Cole. *Making Native Space: Colonialism, Resistance, and Reserves in British Columbia.* Vancouver: UBC Press, 2002.

Huu-ay-aht First Nations. "Kiix?in Agenda Paper." In Alan L. Hoover, ed. *Nuu-chah-nulth Voices, Histories, Objects & Journeys.* Victoria: Royal BC Museum, 2000.

McMillan, Alan D. *Since the Time of the Transformers: The Ancient Heritage of the Nuu-chah-nulth, Dididaht, and Makah.* Vancouver: UBC Press, 1999.

Scott, R. Bruce. *Bamfield Years: Recollections.* Victoria: Sono Nis Press, 1986.

———. *Barkley Sound: A History of the Pacific Rim National Park Area.* Victoria: Sono Nis Press, 1972.

Unpublished or Archival Records

Blenkinsop, George. Reports submitted to the Department of Indian Affairs, 1874. Ottawa, RG 10. National Archives of Canada.

Canada Census, 1881. Returns for Vancouver Island.

Carmichael, Alfred. "Field Notes Relating to Kee'hin," n.d. MS 2305. BC Archives.

Dennis, Robert J. "Chief Louie Nookmiis—First Draft Translation of his Oral History." Prepared for Huu-ay-aht First Nation, 1998.

Francis, Peter, and W.E. Banfield. "Correspondence: Peter Francis and W.E. Banfield to James Douglas." Colonial Correspondence, GR 1372, file 588a/2, 1855. BC Archives.

Guillod, Harry. Extract from diary November 2, 1868. Published in *Eleventh annual report of the Columbia Mission for the year 1869.*

Inglis, Richard L., and James C. Haggarty. "Pacific Rim National Park Ethnographic History." Unpublished manuscript. 1986.

O'Reilly, Peter. Diary. 1882. MS 2894. BC Archives.

Prevost, James. "Letter of Proceedings: Prevost to de Courcy, 11 March 1859." Colonial Correspondence, GR 1372, file 1218, 1859. BC Archives.

Royal Commission on Indian Affairs for the Province of British Columbia. Transcripts of Testimony, 1914. MS 1995. BC Archives.

Sapir, Edward. Nootka Material. Franz Boaz Collection. American Philosophical Society Library.

Index

Acknowledgements

First and foremost, we acknowledge the Huu-ay-aht elders, whose sense of purpose in recounting the histories and preserving traditional knowledge has ensured continuity for their people. In particular, Chief Louie Nookmiis was pivotal in bridging the generations. He was born and grew up in a transitional time and understood his importance as a link between generations before and after.

Thanks are also offered to Huu-ay-aht chiefs and council for their support of this project, in particular, Chief Tliishin Spencer Peters (deceased), Robert Dennis Sr. and Jeff Cook.

About the Authors

Kathryn Bridge is an archivist and historian who lives in Victoria. She has written several books about pioneers in British Columbia, including *By Snowshoe, Buckboard and Steamer: Women of the Frontier* (winner of the Lieutenant Governor's Medal for Historical Writing) and *A Passion for Mountains: The Lives of Don and Phyllis Munday* (a finalist at the Banff Mountain Book Festival). She has also edited first publications of Emily Carr's *Wild Flowers* and *Sister and I* and curated major exhibitions of the artist's life and art. Kathryn recently completed her PhD in Canadian history with a dissertation about diaries and letters written by children in 19th-century western Canada.

Kevin Neary is a consultant in anthropology, research and museum interpretation for many First Nations and cultural institutions in British Columbia. He has participated in several research projects with the Huu-ay-aht over the past 20 years, developing a warm appreciation for Huu-ay-aht people, culture, language and history. Kevin has researched and written many cultural history reports for the Huu-ay-aht and other First Nations in BC, is an author of several anthropological articles and a co-author of the popular Royal BC Museum *Legacy* exhibit catalogue.